Witchcraft Therapy

YOUR GUIDE TO BANISHING BULLSH*T AND INVOKING YOUR INNER POWER

Mandi Em

ADAMS MEDIA

NEW YORK   LONDON   TORONTO   SYDNEY   NEW DELHI

Adams media

Adams Media
An Imprint of Simon & Schuster, Inc.
100 Technology Center Drive
Stoughton, Massachusetts 02072

First Adams Media hardcover
edition May 2021

ADAMS MEDIA and colophon are
trademarks of Simon & Schuster.

For information about special
discounts for bulk purchases, please
contact Simon & Schuster Special
Sales at 1-866-506-1949 or
business@simonandschuster.com.

The Simon & Schuster Speakers
Bureau can bring authors to your
live event. For more information
or to book an event contact the
Simon & Schuster Speakers Bureau
at 1-866-248-3049 or visit our
website at www.simonspeakers.com.

Interior design by Julia Jacintho
Interior images © 123RF/artnis,
Antonina Bilobrovska, Nadezda
Makushkina, Varvara Gorbash,
abirvalg, roystudio

Manufactured in Canada

10 9 8 7 6 5 4 3

Library of Congress Cataloging-
in-Publication Data has been
applied for.

ISBN 978-1-5072-1583-8
ISBN 978-1-5072-1584-5 (ebook)

DEDICATION

To David,
who builds me ladders
when my dreams
feel out of reach.

CONTENTS

Chapter Two

CONJURE CONFIDENCE ... 59

Chapter Three

SUMMON CALM ... 91

Chapter Four

MAKE MENTAL HEALTH MAGIC ... 121

Chapter Five

CAST RELATIONAL SORCERY ... 157

Chapter Six

ENCHANT YOUR LIFE ... 189

INDEX ... 218

INTRODUCTION

Stuck in a situation that's draining your happiness? Struggling with anxious thoughts that talk you out of going after what you want? Wishing you could conjure real, lasting confidence in yourself and your abilities?

Well, guess what: You *can* unstick yourself. You *can* claim what you deserve, and you *can* realize just how much you have to offer—with a little help from the mystical forces of intention, divination, and mindful manifestation. At its core, practicing magic is a formidable source of empowerment: It is a path to own your shit and use all of the resources available to you to create the reality you want. The cornerstones of witchcraft aren't Mason jars and splattered bits of wax: They are personal growth, healing, and a respectful reverence for the natural world and your unique place within it.

And *Witchcraft Therapy* is here to serve as your guide, helping you navigate the constant twists and turns that life churns out, by using witchcraft as a tool for not just staying afloat, but also for dominating whatever comes your way. This book takes the problematic things that life tosses up and gives you magical solutions for taking your power back. You'll find fifty activities to work through common challenges, organized under the chapter themes of mindset, confidence, calm, mental health, relationships, and success and motivation. Each entry explores a problem in more detail, explains just how fucking magical you are when it comes to overcoming it, and prescribes a spell, ritual, or other exercise to heal your troubles. As a science-seeking witch, I've been skeptical myself of certain parts of the craft (looking at you, manifestation), and that's why this book approaches concepts and magical workings in a practical, analytical way.

Just be warned: This isn't a journey through warm fuzzies and empty "live, laugh, love" inspirations. The mark of a truly powerful spellcaster is the ability to recognize how much agency you have over your own life. You're about to dig deep, root around in the shadows, and banish the bullshit that doesn't deserve the space it's keeping in your head and your heart. Are you ready to connect with the badass witch inside of you?

MAGICAL BASICS

So you want to invoke your inner witch and manifest the life you truly desire. But first, some ground rules. And by rules, I'm not talking about any rigid "do this or else you aren't a true witch" bullshit: These are simply things to keep in mind when using witchcraft as a means to better yourself and your experiences. Although the beauty of witchcraft as a practice is the flexibility and freedom to reclaim personal power in your own life, there are certain fundamentals when it comes to practicing magic that are important to be aware of to harvest the best results. The following sections outline these magical basics, including key takeaways and techniques, in more detail.

Magic and the Mundane

If there's any one piece of wisdom that you gain from this book, especially in the context of wellness witchery, let it be this: You won't get fuck-all if you don't do the work.

Too many folks come into witchcraft believing what they've seen on TV, and it shows. They think they can just recite an incantation, sit back, and watch their desires materialize out of thin air. The reality is magic alone isn't going to sweep in and do all the dirty work for you. Yes, there are countless stories of people (myself included) manifesting amazing things and seeing even the most basic spells summon powerful results, but those practices are never done in isolation. Using magic not as a quick fix but as an amplifier to real-world action is the mark of the truly powerful witch.

Think of it this way: You can perform spells to find employment until you're blue in the face, but your chances of actually getting hired explode exponentially if you're also out there pounding pavement, handing out resumes like it's your job. This works in the healing sense as well. You can do rituals and spells for your own peace of mind over things you can't control, but at the end of the day if you aren't also watching where your energy and mental efforts are going, you're less likely to push through to a better place.

If you want to use magic to make shit happen, then hell yeah, let's go! However, be careful not to underestimate the magic of the mundane for getting the most powerful results. In putting in the work, you're programming your brain to see the value of your own actions when it comes to grabbing this beautiful, chaotic life by the balls.

Essential Techniques

Although "witch" is more an archetype than a formalized role, there are some essential techniques that feature prominently in most witches' practices. The following is a quick reference guide to these techniques. Each chapter of this book contains one or some combination of these techniques.

Energy Work

Energy work involves developing a sense of the energies swirling all around and within you and training yourself to recognize shifts in these energies. This is especially important to witchcraft, as witches "raise energy" to put toward spell and ritual work. Many witches also hold the belief that the energy of one thing or being can become attached to other objects, places, or people, potentially causing interference with mental states or magical workings. Energy work can get a bad rap for being kind of "out there," but as anyone who's dealt with a sketchy situation or been in the same room with an upset person will attest, energies can most definitely be felt.

Developing your ability to perceive energies is helpful when working with plants, people, and yourself. As you start paying more attention to subtle shifts in energy, you will be more adept at manipulating it for spellwork. This perception and the intentional manipulation of energy are typically achieved through the use of visualization, such as imagining a cleansing light that radiates from the earth up into your physical body. As you begin to note the way(s) this energy feels within your body, you will be able to then focus on directing it where you'd like it to go (for example, through your palms and into an object or spell jar).

Simple actions such as noticing differences in energies as you enter different locations (for example, going from one room to another) can also help you develop your intuition—another strength when developing your craft. Gut feelings are a real thing, and when you do something as subtle as paying attention to the physical sensations and thoughts you have when entering a new space, you're essentially allowing the voice of intuition within you to speak. Many of us have had experiences where we knew when something was amiss in our environment just based on that voice. Although it may take a while to truly get to know and strengthen your intuition, ultimately it's a useful skill that's worth developing. In fact, the two become a cycle of improvement:

As your intuition gets stronger, so, too, will your energetic perceptions, and vice versa. Both of these will help you become an even more successful witch.

Grounding

Grounding is a mindfulness exercise for getting in touch with the earth and yanking you back into the present moment, something that many of us future-fretters and past-dwellers seriously need help doing.

Grounding activities build on your relationship with the earth and bring you back to the present by reconnecting you with the swirling natural energy that's all around you. In modern life, this energy is largely neglected, as many of us are glued to our devices 24/7 and stuck in the soul-sucking vortex of working for the man as we struggle in an every-man-for-himself society. In an energetically disconnected state, you are likely to be wound up and anxious, causing your energy to become unbalanced and difficult to focus. Through grounding, you get reacquainted with your energy and the energies around you.

In the context of witchcraft, grounding is commonly done pre– and post–magical work as a way to help raise and direct your energy to what you're trying to accomplish. That being said, even non-witchy types can benefit from incorporating grounding practices into their daily routine. At its core, grounding is a type of mindfulness practice, and you'd be hard-pressed to find an adult that wouldn't benefit from being more present in the here and now. Research proves that people who live mindfully are typically calmer, happier, and more tapped in to their feelings. Which is a far better way to live than getting hung up fretting about the past or stressing about the future.

Although there are many grounding techniques, some of the most effective involve connecting to the energy of the earth in a physical way, such as putting your bare feet in the grass. Grounding is like a sister practice to other mindfulness exercises such as meditation, and some everyday activities such as hiking and gardening that incorporate different elements of mindfulness are incredibly grounding.

Manifestation/Intention Setting

Manifestation and the act of setting an intention are hugely important in witchcraft. In fact, most spells and rituals incorporate these in some way to get the results that the practitioner is seeking. Essentially, they attempt to transmute your desires into your reality by providing a focus for where your thoughts and energy go, both during spellwork and as you move throughout your day.

The legendary Law of Attraction is the philosophical basis for manifestation techniques: It states that your thoughts and energy can direct what manifests in the physical plane. Similarly, intention setting runs on the premise that if you choose to direct your energy toward your intentions, you're on your way to turning beliefs into tangible things. They are the essence of bending what *is* into what you desire it to *be*. Even if you hold a skeptical view toward this element of craft as I did, the act of setting intentions or directing your energy can be viewed as a psychological tool to glean real-world results through focus, drive, and dedication.

Journaling

Journaling is one of the best ways to connect with your inner self and nail down your intentions in a concrete way. Bonus: Journaling can be an incredibly therapeutic tool, whether it be freewriting, writing through your emotions, or using structured prompts. Journaling is often recommended by counselors and therapists for boosting creativity and working through complex emotions.

Although the most well-known journals when it comes to witchcraft tend to be the grimoire (a magical recipe book with instructions for practicing the craft) or book of shadows (similar to a grimoire but including more personalized content and notes), other forms of writing and journaling are also beneficial. For example, shadow work, where a person attempts to get in touch with repressed aspects of themselves, is often tackled by way of a journaling practice like freewriting. Other uses for journaling can include tracking goals, moods, and gratitude. Great news for anyone who loves collecting notebooks, as witchcraft will have you filling these up in no time!

Creating Magical Spaces

Creating magical space is important for witches to ensure an environment that is effective for casting spells, performing rituals, etc. There are many different ways to accomplish this, though two of the most well known are casting circles and calling corners. In circle casting, the practitioner creates an energetic boundary around the space they will be working in. A physical circle may also be made from elements such as stones or salt to set a visible boundary for the circle. To call corners, the practitioner invokes the four directions of the earth (north, east, west, and south) and the elements or elemental spirits that correspond with them (earth, air, water, and fire, respectively). Both of these techniques are meant to protect the witch's workings by creating a sacred, protected space. From a secular viewpoint, creating a magical space can act as a psychological prompt to help the practitioner get into the right headspace for spellwork.

Although many witches do not cast circles or call corners, setting the intention for a space to be cleared for magical work is very important. For witches, various forms of energetic cleansing can serve the same purpose to prepare for magical work. How this is accomplished will depend on what feels right for you. Some toss a little salt around and call it a day, while others invoke smoke cleansing with sage or herb bundles and use chants or other higher-level ritualistic practices.

Ultimately, the purpose is to create, even if only psychologically, a space where you are dedicated to the work you're about to do. This space should be free of any funky energies, either that already exist there or that you're bringing to the table (hello, grounding), and should be very clearly set up for the ritual work you're about to do.

Meditation and Visualization

These techniques are essential for training your mind to help your will manifest in the meatspace (a.k.a. physical world) as you practice magic. Meditating can quiet your mind of all the chatter so you can focus on your desires and connect to your inner wisdom and has been scientifically proven to have tons of health benefits including reducing stress and helping with physical ailments such as chronic pain. Visualization can be used in a similar way and has the added bonus of helping you get mega familiar with what you want your life to look like. It can be used hand in hand with manifesting and intention setting, as a tool to imagine yourself in a place where the things you want have already happened.

Rituals

Ritual work is important because it allows you to put your life on autopilot when you just can't even. Instead of trying to muster up more energy and willpower when you already feel spent, you can do something beneficial without even thinking about it. Rituals can also be very calming and help with stress reduction, as they invite a little bit of Zen into your day. Additionally, they are a powerful way to practice simple, everyday mindfulness, bringing you back into the here and now.

Rituals can be as small as stirring intentions into your morning coffee ("I will be a calm and happy kinda witch today") or as elaborate as larger, more complex spellwork. I personally look at more complicated ritual activities as an easy way to hack my brain into getting into a certain mindset. If you've ever participated in more complex ritual work, you may have experienced slipping into an altered or "flow" state. In this state, you may feel an otherworldly sort of connectedness, a very magical vibe, which enables you to focus better on your intentions and directing your energy. In any case, you feel yourself getting into "the zone" for effective magic.

Life can feel incredibly chaotic at times, and there are many areas in which you can feel helpless. Through rituals, you can carve out a sense of agency and inject a little more predictability into your life. And these benefits are there for *anyone* regardless of worldview. Which is great news for my fellow skeptical/secular witches.

Notes about Safety

Although wearing flowing robes surrounded by candles is a whole vibe, burning your house down isn't. Take it from a clumsy witch with experience in the matter: Stay safe! Never leave candles unattended, be very careful when it comes to water safety (e.g., don't drink a bottle of wine then fall asleep in the tub during a ritual), and only ingest and/or apply herbal substances you've gotten from a trustworthy source. Additionally, if you're going to be using smoke cleansing, make sure you consider the lung health of any kids and pets nearby. Read safety tips and warnings on your magical ingredients and tools carefully and follow recommendations for use.

As an addendum to the previous point about real-world action, it's important to recognize that spellwork is best used alongside proper medical advice. Please don't merely light a candle for a severed forearm and hope for the best. Wafting palo santo smoke isn't an effective treatment for a herniated spleen or mental disorder. Regardless of how you feel toward Western medicine, sometimes going to a doctor or therapist is *the most effective* ritual. The same applies for interpersonal safety. While hexing someone who's harmed you might feel like an effective plan, getting yourself out of a bad situation and to a safe space can be the greatest spell for the highest good.

Go Forth and Make Magic

Now that you've explored basic practices for the craft, you're ready to tackle the magical work in the following chapters. As you continue through this book, it's important to remember that witchcraft is not a set of rules and spells so much as it is a way of approaching life. It's a method for hacking the mundane in order to overcome all of life's bullshit in ways that make you feel empowered. It's a course to personal growth.

Chapter One

VIBE CHECK

YOUR

MINDSET

Your beliefs and how you view both yourself and the world can hugely influence the way you experience and navigate this bitch of a life. Does your outlook pass the vibe check? The truth is that many drift through life with the kind of mindset that does nothing but drag them down. We carry limiting beliefs about ourselves, the world, and what is possible. These leave us doubtful of our abilities, feeling negatively about what exists around us, and often unwilling to even try going after the things we want. To vibe check your mindset—a.k.a. break down these beliefs one by one and realize your power over your reality—is to take the first step toward healing your life.

Witchcraft can be an incredibly powerful tool for working on your mindset, as it encourages taking time for personal growth and stresses the importance of individual power. By adopting the simple witchy practices in this chapter that help you connect with the self, you'll find yourself able to forge little moments of calm and gratitude in the clusterfuck of everyday modern life. You'll finally stop shit-talking yourself and challenge the myth that you're helpless in your own storyline. Although an attitude adjustment can't cure *all* problems, to work on your mindset is to essentially shift the way you approach life. Much like witchcraft itself, it can be a truly transformative element for amplifying your happiness, growth, and resilience.

Get Your Grounding Game on Point:
Energetically Aligning with the Earth

One day you're young and carefree, and the next you find yourself crying over the Folgers holiday commercial because adulthood is a mess and what is life even?

We humans are deeply emotional creatures, and whether you're skeptical of "energy work" or not, it's unquestionable that we carry the emotional toll of our experiences with us through life as negative energy. This is a totally normal thing, of course, and everyone copes with this baggage differently, but to be honest, most people can benefit from doing a little grounding work to get to a more energetically balanced place when emotions are becoming overwhelming.

Grounding and centering can be an antidote to the daily overload of what-the-fuckery that leaves you wound up, disconnected, and internally screaming. While there are many ways to go about grounding yourself, each involves the act of participating in a healing energy exchange with the earth.

Now, you might be thinking "An energy exchange with the earth? What's she on about?" and for that I wouldn't blame you. I know it sounds very woo-woo, the kind of thing that a caftan-clad woman with a bra loaded full of crystals would say casually before proclaiming your toxic trait is "having a Scorpio moon" (as I shake an amethyst out of my bra), but I promise you that even the harshest skeptics among us can't refute the fact that there is literally no downside to engaging in an exercise that calls upon us to stand in the woods, put our feet in the grass, stop, breathe, and just *pause*.

I'm probably the most high-strung, overthinky sack of crazy you'll ever meet, and my own life shifted dramatically from simply taking 5–10 minutes every night to sit in the grass alone and ground myself. Although this technique is used in witchcraft pre- and post-ritual work, or during those times that you are positively brimming with internal chaos, I've also found it to be an immensely gratifying way to cap off any day.

Think about it: Most of us spend our days glued to our various screens, working hard for the things we have, and endlessly barraged with bad news that makes us feel equal parts helpless and hopeless. For the most part, our modern society is completely separated from the natural world, set up in a way that makes it hard for people to even find the time to get off the hamster wheel of infinite responsibility and escape into natural spaces. All of this just sucks us further into the loop of disconnection and anxiety, which then fuels the shitty feelings that many of us experience on a daily basis.

It's madness.

That's why, whether you're a seasoned sorceress or an eager new witchling, working on perfecting your grounding game is an exercise that is well worth your time and energy. In the end, when life gets challenging, just take a deep breath, stretch out your arms, and then curl up on the ground and desperately beg the earth to reclaim you!

A Grounding and Centering Exercise (with an Urban Witch Adaptation)

Get outside and find a safe, quiet area to complete the following steps:

1. Sit down and place your feet (bare if possible) and palms on the ground.

2. Start doing some deep breathing and visualize a small seed of light in the core of your body.

3. As you breathe, imagine that seed growing roots that branch out through your body, traveling down your arms and legs, through your palms and the soles of your feet and into the ground.

4. With each exhale, visualize the negative energy from the seed flowing into the ground, where it is cleansed.

5. With each inhale, imagine this cleansed energy as white light you pull back up into yourself through the roots of the seed.

6. Continue steps 4 and 5, imagining yourself as forming a loop with the earth that is essentially acting as an energetic filter, filling you up with healing energy.

7. Stop when you feel energetically realigned.

It's important to recognize that not everybody has convenient and available access to nature, so this practice can be adapted. Yards and gardens are a privilege, and accessing public lands and parks can be difficult for some. The following is an adapted grounding exercise for city dwellers:

1. Sit on the floor of your living space in a cross-legged position. If you have houseplants, sit in a room with plants. If you don't, simply hold an item that has natural significance, such as a rock or stick you've picked up in your travels.

2. Start the breathing exercise outlined previously, picturing the energy of your houseplant(s) flowing through your pores and into your core. When you exhale, imagine your energy being released into your living space to be cleansed.

3. If you are holding a rock or stick, do the same exercise but imagine the energy exchange flowing between the item and your palms.

Challenge the Helplessness Myth:
Manifesting the Life You Want

To know a witch, much less be one, is to know a person who is very well acquainted with manifestation. After all, manifestation and intention setting are two of the most important components of spellcrafting.

"Manifestation" is a concept that's usually talked about in the context of the Law of Attraction, probably the most famous and buzzworthy of the Universal Laws (a collection of "laws" about how the Universe works that can be traced back to ancient cultures). According to the Law of Attraction, your thoughts have the power to manifest in your physical reality. It's believed that by shifting the quality of your energy and changing your mental outlook and perspective, you can essentially create what it is you are seeking out of life.

It may sound crazy, I know. As a die-hard skeptic and science-seeking witch, this concept was challenging for me to understand and trust in at first. Although there is sound scientific support for the power of mind over matter, the idea of "vibes" and "trusting the Universe" hit me in all the wrong places. It sounded like nothing more than fluffy, pseudoscientific nonsense. However, at a particularly low point in my life I decided what the hell and began a manifestation routine that I haven't dropped since. During that low point, I was feeling so helpless that I longed for anything that would help me feel some sort of agency over the things in my life that truly felt uncontrollable. Manifestation did that plus some—radically changing my life until every single thing that I was trying to create became a reality.

So I began to wonder: What if things are not as helpless as they seem? Tears are emotion made physical, and stress-caused illness can show us the power of the mental manifesting in the physical world. To create is a manifestation, ideas plucked seemingly out of the ether and brought to life with the artist as the channel. Perhaps it is possible to love the idea of objective truth, while still remaining open to the possibility of magic?

For me, dropping the desire to know how manifestation worked and simply allowing myself to sink deep into the wonderful magic of the results was a game-changer. Instead of getting caught up in questions of why and how, I jumped in headfirst. Like with all spellwork, I matched my manifestations with real-world action, and kept at it until I saw results. I claimed a power and control I had been denying myself. At the end of the day, even if it's simply the dance between coincidence and the placebo effect (and I'm not convinced that it is), I no longer felt helpless.

The cornerstones of manifestation are defining a goal, using real-world action, letting go of control over the outcome, and having a positive outlook in regard to that outcome. In doing these things, regardless of your spirituality or worldview, you can create a life that aligns with the things you want. You can stop helplessness in its tracks and make shit happen. So hop to it!

As an important sidenote, it's imperative that any conversation about "thoughts creating reality" holds space for the very real interconnected web of chaos that characterizes life on this planet. Too many times people are blamed for their wounds and traumatic experiences, as if they didn't try hard enough or do enough to manifest a reality that was better. You can miss me with all of that. That stuff didn't happen to you because your vibes were off, and to suggest as much is toxic spirituality at its finest. Don't ever forget it.

A Manifestation Routine

Follow these steps to bring your own manifestation magic to life:

1. Figure out what your goal is, or what you're trying to attract. Be very specific.

2. Dig deep into why you want this. Where are your intentions coming from? Is it a good place? Although this might seem like an unnecessary step, it's very important. Most of the time when we don't see our manifestations work out, it's because something within this step was off. For example, if you are trying to manifest something you think should be in your life, but deep down you don't really want it, you'll likely be hit with resistance.

3. Write down your goal/desire in terms of it definitely happening. For example, when I was hoping to move to an area that seemed unattainable for various reasons, I started writing in my journal, "I will relocate to *X* region, find a job that helps me qualify for a mortgage, and find a house within my price range that checks all the necessary boxes." I did this daily, matching this written statement of intent with real-world action, and within six months it was done.

4. Take at least a few minutes nightly to visualize your goal/desire as if it's already happened, skipping forward to the end where it is already realized. For example, if you want to manifest writing a book, visualize yourself holding your book in print.

5. Feel gratitude for receiving this thing that you wanted. Let the feeling of it actually wash over you.

6. Trust that it will truly happen if it's for the highest good, and try not to get too concerned about the when or how. Truly attempt to forget about it and give yourself a break from wanting it so bad. You don't need that needy energy. You can relax in knowing that in the future, this shit has already happened. Boom!

Bonus: Because all magical work requires real-world action, do the following to ramp up your results:

1. Shake up your routine to holler at the Universe that you're willing and open to change.

2. Make moves as if you've already received the thing you wanted (for example, prior to making my big move, I bought a car that could handle the weather where I intended to live).

3. Believe in yourself and trust the Universe.

Flip Your Mindset by Being Grateful AF:
Taking Stock of the Things That Don't Suck

Ever-obnoxious advice to "live, laugh, love" aside, practicing gratitude is a very important, worthwhile skill. Not only will it help you get in the right headspace to see success in your personal spells and manifestations; it also has hella health benefits (research shows it can improve the quality of your sleep, enhance your self-esteem, and promote resilience) and can literally transform the way your brain works. Not to mention that other people may find you more likable, because the truth is nobody likes being around a whiny sad sack. And that's a *fact*. By adopting a gratitude mindset, you can watch a negative attitude transform from an unhappy little caterpillar to a glorious "shit isn't so bad" kinda butterfly!

This is a topic that is very special to me, because my own mental inclinations have always leaned heavily to the negative side. So in my experience, the quest for a gratitude mindset was hard AF—but utterly life-changing. Once I began to master this skill, everything in my life began to change for the better. Bang for your buck, shifting your mindset to a place of gratitude has some of the greatest returns when it comes to making lasting changes in your overall outlook on life *and* yourself.

In Buddhism there is the concept known as the "hungry ghost." Hungry ghosts are wretched creatures; they have large bellies and thin, pinhole throats that don't allow them to eat, so they remain unsatiated, eternally hungry for more. Although there is various lore and significance attached to this particular concept, the hungry ghost serves to caution us of the dangers that arise from the endless want for more.

How does this play into gratitude exactly? For many people it's second nature to look at the glass as being half empty, pushing us to seek for more and more to fill it with. Instead of recognizing what exists in the cup, we see a void, and the desire to fill it can keep us in a state of constant gnawing hunger—much like the hungry ghost. So, when we ask ourselves what to feel grateful for, all we see is a barren wasteland of lack, surrounded by mountains of pain and trauma, and it can be hard to identify the potential for joy and abundance in our lives.

However, this tendency doesn't necessarily come from a place of greed. If you're a person who's experienced deeply negative transformative experiences, you can ultimately end up forming a blind spot when it comes to seeking the bright side. As an adaptive response, trauma keeps you hardwired to notice immediate threats and shortcomings so that you can mentally prepare yourself in order to survive. Meanwhile, the good things are left unrecognized. But it doesn't have to be this way.

At the end of the day, even the most miserable bastards among us have things they could undoubtedly be grateful for: the ability to think and make decisions, to feel the sun on your skin, the fact that you entered this world as a human that can eat delicious foods and watch *Netflix*. There are things to be grateful for all around you.

Training your brain to be grateful has an immensely important place in witchcraft specifically for a few reasons. First off, the path of the witch is one of personal growth and development.

This means that in dedicating yourself to the craft you are committed to stepping into your true power, and there are few things more powerful than mastering your own brain. Additionally, having the ability to slip into a state of unconditional gratitude will prove extremely helpful for your manifestation work, rituals, and spells. Ultimately, a gratitude mindset aligns your personal energy to the outcome that you're looking for. In witchy terms, this means getting them results! If you want to begin developing your own gratitude practice, the good news is that you can do so in just a few minutes per day. The even better news is that if you do this consistently, chances are it will eventually become second nature, making you a magnet for abundance, happiness, and feel-good energy.

Long story short, adopt a gratitude mindset. Trust me, it's beyond worth it!

A Quick and Dirty Daily Ritual to Become Grateful AF

For this ritual, you'll need:

- A few spare minutes in the morning
- A notebook
- A pen or pencil

1. Take a few minutes in the morning (maybe while you're having your daily cup of tea or coffee) to sit down with your notebook.

2. Take a few deep breaths, then write down at least three things that you can identify gratitude for. As you do this, pause to actually allow the grateful feeling to wash over you,

noting that there may be other feelings that come along with it, such as love, relief, excitement, etc. In the beginning this might be hard. However, if you need to scrape the bottom of the barrel for ideas until this becomes easier, then do it. "I'm grateful to be alive" or "I'm grateful for this coffee" are simple things to start with.

3. As you get more proficient with this ritual, you can start countering complaints that pop up through the day with their grateful counterparts. As long as you begin the process of simply looking for these things to feel thankful for, you'll be well on your way to changing your outlook for the better.

One note: While some people advocate for thinking of things you're grateful for while you're still in bed in the morning, those of us being awakened by the shrill, zero-chill screeching of children are more likely to be letting out a hearty "*Fuck*" than anything even remotely resembling gratitude. If this sounds familiar, give yourself a little time to fully wake up and start the morning before tackling this ritual.

Rid Yourself of Stank-Ass Energy: Cleansing Magic

Cleansing magic is a fundamental cornerstone of modern witch-craft; it's one of the first things that new witchlings are encouraged to become proficient at. The purpose of cleansing is to neutralize or remove unwanted energies from people, items, or surroundings. Similar to a form of protection, cleansing is used for making sure a witch's tools, space, and self are in optimal condition for performing magical works. Cleansing rituals are advised for when you bring new tools into the home (crystals, cards, etc.), prior to performing spells and rituals, or if you've had an experience or intuitive sense that it's needed in order to rebalance energies to a positive or neutral place.

There are infinite ways to perform a cleansing, depending on what your purpose is. Cleanses can be using salt, burning herbs, burying objects, taking a reflective shower, floor washes—the possibilities are endless. The trick is to be in touch with why the cleanse is needed and go from there to determine the best way to approach it.

The practical benefit of cleansing is to realign energies. And whether you hold a worldview that supports more esoteric ideas about energy or not, we all can relate to that feeling of needing to shake up our vibes. When we find ourselves getting sucked under the tide of some heavy negative shit, it can be far too easy for those events to influence our mindset in a negative way. Emotionally draining life events, periods of illness or depression, or having to spend time with people who bring us down—

these are all precursors to the accumulation of stank-ass energy that we'd be wise to rid ourselves of, quick!

But again, all magical works must be matched by real-world action. You can whip up herbal floor washes, burn sage, and rub yourself down with eggs till even Mr. Clean would approve your aura, but the truth is we all have a responsibility to protect ourselves in mundane ways as well. Just because the bad vibes are there doesn't mean you have to wear them. Recognizing sources of negativity and really focusing on whether these things deserve to take up space is an essential part of creating a magical life.

In this sense, cleansing is the perfect example of the marriage between magic and mundane, as your real-world cleansing efforts can invite magic into your surroundings in a very ordinary way. Just as lighting a bundle of rosemary or sprinkling salt in the corners of your home can be a cleanse, so, too, can re-examining the things in your life and making the necessary adjustments to harmonize your energies. Taking steps to protect yourself from abusive situations is a cleanse, as is saying no to the things that make you uncomfortable and letting go of the harmful things that you're holding on to. This is the real beauty of witchcraft: Despite the portrayal of it as a dramatic, spooky sort of practice, real-life witchery is subtle, powerful, and radically connected to wellness.

Far more than an *Instagram* image of perfectly manicured fingers wafting a cloud of palo santo, cleansing is the act of assertively tackling that which doesn't pass the vibe check—like energetic alchemy that has the power to turn that which is heavy into something more manageable.

A Simple Cleansing Practice to Realign Your Energy

Although there are many different types of cleanses, the following is one that is accessible to most, as it doesn't generate smoke or require too many materials.

For this cleansing practice, you'll need:

- A handheld bell
- Salt
- Water
- 1 slice lemon
- A pinch dried rosemary leaves*
- A spray bottle

1. Open the windows in your living space and ring the bell (banging a spoon on a pot is a valid substitute if you don't have a bell).

2. Clean up some of the clutter in your space.

3. Sprinkle a tiny bit of salt in each room, particularly in the corners and entryways.

4. Fill a medium pot halfway with water, then add lemon, rosemary, and a pinch of salt. Simmer over medium heat until the water is fragrant, then strain and let cool until room temperature.

5. Pour infused water into the spray bottle. Spray around each room, visualizing the mist as neutralizing any of the negative energies that may be present.

6. Sit down and ground yourself, then think about all the positive feelings that you want to invite into your space. Really allow yourself to feel these things, as if they are already happening.

7. Affirm to yourself that your space is cleansed, and that the Universe will fill that space with abundance and blessings.

*Rosemary is a practical ingredient that most people have on hand (it can also make your whole house smell like focaccia bread, which is magic AF).

Be Gentle with Your Trauma:
Holding Space to Treat Your Wounds

Modern spirituality can quickly descend into a pissing contest of who can be more forgiving, more loving, more *positive* in the face of troubles, and although those are great goals and inspo-meme fodder, the truth is that this mindset of undiscerning (a.k.a. toxic) positivity is not an effective salve for the wounds we carry.

This should go without saying, but if bad things have happened to you it has nothing to do with your vibes, your worldview, or the amount of effort you've put into your growth. Although we all have a tendency to suffer from the consequences of our own actions, some things are completely and totally beyond our control. To be alive is to be part of the great sea of human experience—random, swirling, and sometimes violent. No matter where your spiritual beliefs lie, sometimes shit *just happens*. And you can carry the scars for as long as it takes for them to heal.

Much like the experience itself, trauma is difficult to define. It can arise from a single event, ongoing abuse, or even from systemic exposure to traumatizing things. It can be concretely tied to a particular thing, or it can even be vague, such as the trauma that comes from marginalization.

When dealing with these wounds, it's important to get one thing straight real quick: Trauma and emotional pain are entirely subjective. Other people cannot define your experiences or judge the marks that they've made upon you. When dealing with trauma, there's no room for comparisons, judgment, or expectations regarding the "right" way to heal. Despite a current cultural climate that favors toxic positivity and the use of spirituality to bypass negative emotions, the very best thing you can do for your own emotional recovery is to hold space for your trauma and pains, rather than invalidating them and "pushing through." You can recognize that lingering in pain may not be serving you while still giving yourself the loving patience to heal from it on your own terms.

Magic can be a wonderful tool in the healing process, as at its core it's about empowerment. Many of the interpersonal traumas we experience arise from a violation or imbalance of power, and in the craft, we can find some means to transmute those pains as a way to take power *back*. However, a truly wise witch also knows the critical importance of help and safety. Reach out for support, raise your voice, and get professional or legal help if necessary. On an individual level, allow your feelings to make themselves known, and do engage in shadow work if you feel resilient enough to do so. Treat yourself with patience, kindness, and love without blame.

A Trauma Poppet to Shower with Care

In essence, this is much like those "treat an egg like a baby" exercises they gave you in grade school, except this one is a reminder to treat *yourself* with tenderness—to give yourself care and love, and to say all the things you think you need to hear.

To create your own poppet, you'll need:

- 2 large pieces of fabric or felt
- Scissors
- A needle and thread
- Cotton balls and/or dried lavender or rose herbs
- A few strands of your hair
- Rose quartz (optional)

1. To create the poppet, take the pieces of fabric/felt and lay them on top of one another. Cut out the shape of the doll you want to make, then sew the sides and top together.

2. Use the opening at the bottom to stuff the doll with the cotton or herbs and your hair (or other small item that symbolizes "you"). Add rose quartz if desired to symbolize high-vibe self-love.

3. Sew the bottom shut.

4. Hold the poppet in your hand and affirm that it is an extension of you. Imagine your energy radiating out from your heart into your arms, through your hands, and into the doll. Allow yourself to feel the emotions as they come, making sure to ground yourself afterward to rebalance.

5. Sleep with the poppet under your pillow for at least one night to solidify the bond.

6. Once you have bonded with your poppet, place it somewhere that is readily accessible to you. Treat it like an extension of yourself, taking care to speak to it kindly and hold it gently, giving it the respect and love that you would want from another to support you in healing.

This poppet can be taken out during emotional moments, shadow work, or just when you want a visual cue to remind you that you're a person too! The ultimate purpose is to create a proxy by which you can hold space for yourself and your healing.

Fix Your Morning Routine:
Starting the Day Off Like Someone Who's Got Their Shit Together

If you're anything like me, you're a sucker for those articles like "10 Ways to Be More Productive" and "The Exact Routine That Makes All Those Rich Guys So Mega Successful." Maybe it seems like an out-of-reach fantasy—a vacation from "real life." And yes, part of what has helped make some people successful may be luck and/or opportunities a lot of us just don't have access to. But there is one thing they all have in common: a solid morning routine.

While waking up and grabbing your phone to see what your ex is doing, or watching your crazy relatives fight on *Facebook* might seem like a good mental breakfast, turns out it's actually not! The way you spend the first bit of your day can hugely determine the energy and mindset you bring into the rest of it. Which means you have the potential to be a lot happier, healthier, and more productive if you start off on a good foot.

What do you mean stop doomscrolling for three hours first thing in the morning and do something more productive?! That's impossible! Routine is similar to other healthy habits in the sense that we may know it's good for us, and yet we still can't seem to pull ourselves out of the vortex of doing absofuckinglutely nothing to implement it. As creatures of habit, you'd think it would be easier to establish a decent routine, yet it can feel so *difficult*. It's like the habit version of "I'll start my diet tomorrow," where tomorrow never comes.

The reason that most routines fail is the same reason most diets fail: We have a serious thirst for instant gratification, so we rarely do the tedious groundwork necessary for success in new, good habits. After all, what's the fun in starting off slowly, baby step by baby step, when you can just say, "Screw patience," go balls to the wall, get frustrated, and quit, amirite?

If you want to start a better morning routine the first step is to think of what you're trying to achieve. Are you trying to be calmer? Or more positive? Maybe you want to boost your creativity? Now, take your goals and work backward, using them as a guide to determine what things you should be doing in the a.m. to take your life from random chaos to focused magic. Is it taking a walk to de-stress? Gratitude journaling to feel more hopeful about the present? Freewriting to get those creative juices flowing?

Do some soul searching on what you think an ideal routine would be and tackle it in itty-bitty steps. For example, if you want to start a morning walking routine, your first step might be to set your alarm a little earlier each day, or to prepare your clothes the night before. Like a baby colt, you can wobble-leg yourself to success as long as you keep your wits about you and just keep moving. Breaking things down into micro-mini pieces eases some of the pressure and relieves expectations. It's an infinitely better way to take on the whole task without burning out.

Establishing a proper morning routine is a powerful spell. If approached seriously with the right intent and motivation, you can manifest truly incredible things.

I believe in you.

An Easy Witchy Morning Routine

The following is my own magical morning routine in detail; you can either follow this full routine as is, tweak it however you want, or include one or two elements in your own routine.

- When you wake up, take a few deep breaths to ground yourself for the upcoming day.

- Choose a crystal to keep on your person (a pocket or bra works well!) to help cope with whatever you have going on that day. For example, if you're going on a date you might choose rose quartz.

- If you have a tarot deck, ask it what to focus on for the day and pull a single card. Pay attention to what your intuition tells you about the interpretation of the card, and don't panic. For example, my deck gives me The Tower so frequently I'm half wondering if there are sixty Towers in the deck! That being said, I often interpret it as a reminder not to catastrophize, or to keep in mind the importance of going with the flow, rather than a sign of danger ahead.

- Stir intention into your morning cup of tea or coffee. Clockwise motions *add* an intention ("I will be calm today"), and counterclockwise motions *remove* some aspect ("I will be free of doubt today").

- Sit down with your journal and write out some goals and things you are grateful for. Write out your goals as if their success is inevitable: "I will complete the project today."

Write out your gratitude, allowing yourself to feel the positive emotions that come with being thankful AF.

- If you have the space or opportunity, go outside for even a couple of minutes, put your feet in the grass, and take deep breaths. The day may hammer you with petty, insignificant drama, but to be grounded to the earth is to see above the crap. Just two minutes daily can result in a significant attitude adjustment.

Unleash Your Unique Possibilities:
You Are Not Stuck

Have you ever found yourself in a situation where you felt like literally everything in your life was marinating in a pool of suck, and you simply couldn't figure a way out? Or maybe you've known someone who constantly has dilemmas, as every time you try to brainstorm solutions with them, they chime in about all the ways that there is no possible way that things will get better?

Unfortunately, many people are burdened with an overwhelming feeling of being stuck. Whether this comes from legitimate experiences of getting fucked around by fate, or is simply a belief that became established somewhere along the way, having the feeling that you have no control over the things that happen in life is totally natural, if not fully accurate. Although there may be very real reasons for these roadblocks, chances are you have far more agency than you think. Realizing this power and training yourself to look for evidence of it is a wonderful way to cultivate a mindset of empowerment and positivity.

Now I'm not talking about indiscriminate empowerment or positivity here either. The truth of it is that there are absolutely things you *cannot* do. I won't blow some smoke up your ass that you can "do anything!" because that would be a lie; however, there's an even better chance that you *can* do more things than you're giving yourself credit for. Your mission in life is to discover which is which.

We're ultimately creatures of habit and comfort, which is why we don't give ourselves much resistance when we decide that where we're at right now at this very moment is a good enough place to be, even if we aren't really happy.

However, you are not stuck. You have a great amount of power inside of you that is starved for possibility. Shake your shit up and invite magical things into your life. Things can easily change if you both see it as possible and allow yourself the opportunity to believe it. After all, you can't keep putting the same things in and expect a different result.

Sometimes the best way to rebel against the limits you've placed upon yourself is to simply flip the script: Take a good hard look at the definitive statements that you've adopted as rules and challenge them. What if they aren't actually the facts? What possibilities might you be discounting or ignoring here? Also understand that if there are instances where you truly feel you have no control then there's no harm in doing some manifestation work in order to try to change your circumstances, even if you have doubts. You have nothing to lose, and having a little bit of hope certainly won't leave you worse off.

You are not stuck.

A Spell to Break Free from Feeling Stuck

To complete this spell for getting unstuck, you'll need:

- A white candle
- A match or lighter
- A large bay leaf
- A pen
- A large fireproof bowl

1. Sit down and spend five minutes grounding yourself. Light some incense if it helps you get in the zone.

2. Cleanse your space and light the candle.

3. On the bay leaf, write down the positive counterpart of one of the "rules" that's making you feel stuck. For example, if the rule is "I can't move because I'm unable to find a place I can afford," write down "I will get a new place to live that I am able to afford."

4. Light the bay leaf with the candle (be careful not to burn yourself; bay leaves spark) and drop the leaf into the bowl.

5. Meditate on the candle flame while reaffirming to yourself that you are not stuck, doors open for you easily, and you have the power to change your unique circumstances.

Stop Shit-Talking Yourself:
Words Are Spells

Just like the narrators that prattle along with movies, many of us have an inner voice that never seems to shut up. We talk to ourselves in our minds all day long, but are we saying the right things?

Just as we have the ability to manifest our desires through our words and intentions, we also can be our own worst enemies by constantly flagellating ourselves with a steady stream of negative self-talk. In contrast to the small voice of intuition, this inner critic can be loud AF, constantly piping up with yelps and yodels that are strictly intended to keep you exactly where you feel safe: deep in your comfort zone, knowing your place, and never getting too confident. The louder that limiting voice gets, the quieter you end up actually living, effectively paralyzed by fear and doubt. After all, how many risks are you going to be willing to take when chances are you've convinced yourself of failure before even starting?

Ultimately, turning your attention to getting control over this voice will serve you well. Words are spells, and it's important that you ensure yours are saying the right things—the things that encourage and empower you rather than make you feel incapable or unworthy. For years my own life was limited due to the constraints I had spoken into existence: "I'm too X or Y," "I'm not *this* enough for *that*," "I could never do X," and "I'm not the type of person who Y." This sort of chatter completely bypassed any growth or progress that I made.

To arbitrarily limit yourself is to effectively bind your own success and happiness. Cut that shit out and become your own biggest hype-bitch.

Of course, while cutting out negative self-talk is simple enough to suggest in theory, in practice it can be far more challenging. The voice you harbor may have been there as long as you can remember, and in ways it may have been protective. The inner critic can be helpful for keeping you focused and motivated, and reining you in when you might be going recklessly rogue (for example, when you're thinking of putting all your savings into some get-rich-quick scheme).

However, there's a big difference between the inner voice of reason and a chorus of abuse. Ultimately, catching yourself in the habit of trash-talking yourself is an ongoing process. When you catch yourself imposing limits on yourself and what you are like or what you can do, try to take a moment to think about whether these things are based in truth. Alternatively, if you catch yourself beating yourself up or talking down to yourself, take a moment to counter those hurtful words with something positive.

Really, I'll wait.

Part of the incredible magic of being human is the ability to grow and change. As you live your life, you make many shifts, some dramatic and some you might never even notice. Everyone has the capacity to change their mindset and thus their entire life. All those limits you set at some point based on what was going on became a self-fulfilling prophecy, but you can stop that prophecy in its tracks if you choose to put in the effort.

Just like with the gratitude, you may find yourself hard up for material to praise yourself with at first. But don't worry, boo: You'll get used to being kind to yourself over time. Most of us would be quick to defend ourselves if someone else were to dissect our character, so simply shift that energy inward, and it will eventually become second nature to sing your own praises like a sweet songbird.

And if you're worried that by shifting your focus away from all your imagined shortcomings you'll somehow be setting yourself up for catastrophe (hello, anxiety!), know this: You're more likely to actually *hone* your intuition and inner voice of reason by channeling all that mental energy to a place that serves your highest good rather than draining you with needless negativity. To vibe check your mindset is truly a thing of beauty, and treating yourself as a friend is one of the greatest kindnesses you can give yourself. After all, how can you expect to find wisdom and healing in the world when you're spent from fighting a battle against yourself?

Remember: Your words are spells. Channel their power wisely.

A Honey-Tongued Spell

To complete a spell for shifting mean self-talk to empowering affirmation, you'll need:

- A spoon
- Honey
- A warm cup of herbal tea (preferably something calming, such as chamomile or peppermint)
- A mirror

1. Measure a spoonful of honey and tap it into the cup *without* submerging the spoon in the water.

2. Put the spoon on your tongue. Either in your head or out loud say the following incantation while looking in the mirror: "I choose to speak as if to a friend; sweeten my words, with love I'll send."

3. Use the spoon to stir your tea clockwise a few times.

4. Begin sipping the tea. As you drink, visualize it as a medicine that heals your mind's tongue from talking shit about yourself.

5. Repeat this spell as often as needed in order to silence your inner critic and become your own biggest hype-bitch.

Unplug and Disconnect:
Logging In to the Self

Of all the wretched, low-vibe bullshittery we endure, screens have got to be the most nefarious. Modern life has blurred the lines between work and home, of knowledge and power, and where most of these things intersect is on our screens. We have screens in our homes, screens in our hands, screens on our wrists, and screens in our cars. It's madness!

Now don't get me wrong, I like to stretch out covered in Dorito dust while *Netflix* lulls me to sleep just as much as the next guy, but when I get out in the woods away from the TV and my laptop (and if I can, without trying to capture the whole experience on my cellphone camera), I can clearly sense just how disconnected *being* connected all the time has made me. It becomes noticeable almost immediately.

This mindset of needing to be constantly connected makes our lives so noisy we struggle to hear that tiny voice of the wise and intuitive self within each of us. Instead, all we hear—and see—are the flashy, nonstop notifications, ads, news, and more. Additionally, although scrolling can feel fun or mindless in the moment, it's been linked time and time again with increased anxiety and depression. It's a virtual clusterfuck of feels. And it's easy to make justifications for our reckless dependence on these gadgets: It's for work, or for relationships, or to stay informed. However, the truth is that for most of us, we've crossed the line into being irresponsibly tethered all day to devices that take away from the real action all around us. We miss out on the world *outside* the screen.

One reason why it can be so hard to break these habits is because like many things in life, they are reflective of both good and bad. Social media is a good example, as it can help us stay connected and entertained, and yet it's also so toxic that often it harms us without our awareness. We often begin to compare ourselves to other people's lives and aesthetics to see if we measure up—feeling bad when we inevitably fail to match the edited, ultra-curated images we see. The same goes for being an informed citizen—an admirable quality, but where do we draw the line between questing for knowledge and feeding our anxieties?

We need some damn boundaries.

We've also become so hooked on our devices that our measly attempts to curb our addiction do little to shore up the damage. And we're often praised for it. Workplaces love a responsive employee, and friends love a responsive pal. Given the way we tend to be rewarded for being plugged in all the time, it's no wonder it becomes incredibly hard to find balance.

It's really important to step away from these devices and find some time to just *be*. Surely your email can wait if you sit on your deck with a glass of wine for twenty minutes, or go out for a solo hike?

A simple way to create boundaries in your relationship with your devices is to put limits on your behaviors so that they truly match up with your intentions. For example, if you want to stay informed, then limit yourself to checking the news at only a certain time of day. Additionally, try to be very aware of your emotions when you're on social media.

Creating an unplugging ritual can also be helpful for relieving your anxiety around disconnecting, as you're choosing to make a conscious effort to turn your attention elsewhere. Although it should be as easy as just putting the phone (or iPad, or smartwatch) down, you probably know from experience that shit isn't so simple. By making a ritual out of this practice, you essentially give yourself permission and build a habit. One that may even become as enjoyable a part of your day as your morning coffee—or midafternoon road rage (I kid).

The more time you spend off your devices, the more connected you can become to not only the world around you, but also the one *inside* of you. In the absence of nonstop technological distraction, you can become more mindful and aware of your own inner universe. As a witch, being in touch with your intuition and aware of your energies is a top priority, and unplugging is a great way to plug back in to *yourself*.

An Unplugging Ritual

For this ritual, you'll need:

- A box that's big enough to hold your electronic devices
- A large bowl of water (rainwater or moon water works well for this)
- Some flower petals

1. Double-check your notifications, etc. to ensure that your anxiety can't use this as an excuse to power up again after completing the ritual.

2. Turn off your devices and place them in the box.

3. Affirm to yourself that you are consciously unplugging for *X* amount of time (setting a defined time period—for example, thirty minutes—can help spare you from the discomfort of uncertainty).

4. Place the bowl of water on top of the box. Add the flower petals to the water.

5. As you gaze into the water, remind yourself of the stillness of being disconnected.

6. Take a deep breath and turn your attention toward being very mindful of your body sensations and your surroundings. What do you feel? Hear?

7. Follow this up by going for a walk outdoors if possible, or simply go outside and stare at the moon, allowing yourself to feel fully present in the moment, in the real world. The moon represents our inner wisdom and intuition, making it the perfect partner for contemplating our feelings. Do this step for as long as you need to feel rebalanced.

Chapter Two

CONJURE
CONFIDENCE

Confidence is essential to a healthy self, yet it's something that many struggle with. For those with self-esteem issues, hating yourself can become a competitive sport, and anything and everything can be used as fuel for the fire. From body image to wounds of the past, there seems to be no end to the things that can cause you grief if you're suffering from a lack of self-confidence.

Practicing the craft can help with self-esteem in that the root of spellwork involves discovering and connecting with your own potential. By upholding a doctrine that so heavily advocates for wellness and self-care, witchcraft is inherently geared toward improving confidence. Through magic you can tackle the tricky issues of self-esteem and emotional baggage in a way that's powerful yet gentle. In this chapter, you will use the tools of the craft to build a foundation of confidence that can weather the storms of life. You'll learn to love your body, banish self-doubt, connect with your inner strength, and more. Through the work of healing the self and respecting your unique place in the Universe, you can improve your self-esteem and become truly empowered.

Connect with the Strength Inside:
You Can Do the Hard Shit

Life is full of little tests that you have to somehow get through without passing out from fear. It's like a very mundane video game with the difficulty set to "WTF."

We face a variety of difficult things that can stress us out and drain us of our energy. From simple-ish things like job interviews, to more difficult things like speaking up about a toxic situation or relationship, we're tasked with all sorts of things that cause our chests to tighten and our hearts to beat fast. Nobody said life was easy, but at times it can feel downright fucked.

As a person who's predisposed to anxiety and is severely averse to conflict, any situation that has the potential to be difficult or unpredictable tends to make my blood run cold. In particularly rough periods in the past, I've even been known to tear up from the mere *suggestion* of doing things outside my comfort zone where I had no control over the variables. However, it is possible to get past these fears and self-doubts and find comfort in the fact that when it comes to doing hard shit, you're very well practiced!

Since you rocketed out of the womb and emerged all red and screaming, you've been doing very difficult things. Things you weren't prepared for. Hard stuff happens every day and look: You're still here to tell the tale! Yet somewhere along the line, you may have become so hung up on rejection, embarrassment, and the possibility of failure that you forget just how tough you are when it comes to pushing through.

It's the ultimate act of stubborn avoidance to try to sidestep the hard stuff. What you're actually trying to get away from is those difficult feelings. And fear of facing those emotions is what holds you back and keeps you locked in your safety zone, terrified of doing things that are a stretch for you.

But seriously, if you just take a deep breath and recognize just how powerful you are at facing these challenges, you'd kick that resistance to the curb, puff up your chest, and be ready to take over the world. The resistance that you feel is just a red herring: a distraction that takes focus away from the fire that burns within you. The hard stuff isn't to be avoided; in fact, it's the secret sauce that makes life infinitely juicier. Although it sucks in the moment, every failure, rejection, and embarrassing slip is another chance to learn and grow. These moments are doorways, not closed doors, and by going through them you can find yourself somewhere wonderful and new, your soul nourished by the simple act of taking a chance. There's no law that says you have to be perfect.

So break through the resistance and connect to the fighter within. Look at yourself in the mirror and call yourself a warrior. You are more than capable of doing difficult things, and what's more, you're able to do it scared. And if it doesn't work out then learn from it and move on.

An Enchantment Spell

To complete this spell for inner strength, you'll need:

- An item to be charmed, such as a necklace, bracelet, or pocket charm (even a rock or crystal will do!)
- A small bowl of salt
- Strength tarot card (optional)

1. Lay your item in your bowl of salt. The purpose of this is to cleanse the item, so you can substitute with smoke cleansing or any other preferred cleansing method.

2. Hold your cleansed item in your hands. Breathe deeply, and imagine a white light starting at the area of your third eye (on the forehead, just above and between the eyes) filling your body, flowing through your arms and out of your hands into the charm.

3. Visualize this powerful white light full of strength, courage, and resilience filling the item. If it helps to do so, focus on the Strength tarot card while you do this.

4. Tell the item what its purpose is: to lend you the strength to do hard things.

5. For an added boost, lay your item on top of the Strength card on your windowsill during the next full moon. This will help amp up your enchantment magic.

Although this item is enchanted by magic, the kicker is that its energy is created by *you*. All that strength and courage you have deep inside is getting coaxed out and fortified to act as a shield, making you completely and totally unfuckwithable.

Tap In to Your Intuition:
Tuning In to Your Inner Wise Witch

Have you ever met someone who made your skin crawl, or had a very strong feeling compelling you toward a certain decision? Maybe you even ended up looking back with the realization that your intuition was trying to hijack your awareness!

A strong intuition is profoundly underrated. Many successful people throughout history attributed their good fortune to listening to their gut, yet we still frequently look upon following our intuition as some sort of woo bullshit. All too often we get into conflict with our own gut instincts and end up doubting ourselves rather than listening to the very wise voice inside hollering, "Pay attention!"

Now, intuition is something everyone has, but just how good you are at listening to it can vary dramatically. While some people are highly intuitive in a way that can seem downright freaky, other folks wander through life feeling as if their inner wisdom went out for a pack of smokes and never came back. Wherever you land on the spectrum, you can find comfort by looking at intuition as a skill, which means that you can (and should) develop it.

Anxiety poses an obstacle for many when it comes to listening to and strengthening their intuition. It can be immensely difficult to differentiate between an intuitive sense and your average run-of-the-mill "sky is falling" primal gut scream that's the specialty of the anxious mind. But although it may be difficult to tell the difference between the two, it isn't impossible. By learning to quiet your mind through techniques such as meditation and grounding, you can work to silence your anxious voice, giving way to a louder intuition.

Other techniques that can be used to strengthen your intuition include journaling, documenting your dreams, spending time alone in nature, and trying to incorporate mindfulness into your daily routine. Life hits you fast, and so you tend to not pay enough attention to the signals your body and senses give you. By adopting a more mindful approach to each moment, you may find yourself feeling more connected to your body and able to recognize the little tugs and pulls of the intuitive self.

However, probably one of the most simple and underrated ways to tap in to that intuitive mind is to plainly state your intention. Affirm to yourself, "I am focusing to improve the connection to my intuition." State it to yourself before you go to bed and affirm it to yourself first thing in the morning by writing it down. This will prompt your brain to plug in to the cues that might pop up throughout the day.

Ultimately, in acknowledging the fact that you're open to connecting with your intuition, you're effectively opening the door to receiving its wisdom. Although it takes practice and some honing, the development of a strong intuitive self can reap many rewards in all aspects of your life.

Shut up and let your gut speak!

An Inner Power Ritual

To complete this ritual, you'll need:

- A white candle
- A match or lighter
- A charcoal disc
- A small cauldron or other fireproof vessel
- Frankincense resin
- A journal or sketch paper
- A pen or pencil

1. Start by cleansing your space and grounding yourself.

2. Light the candle and affirm, "This is the spark of intuition; let it light my way."

3. Place the charcoal disc into the cauldron or other vessel and light it. Once the disc is lit (it will be red hot with grey ash) carefully sprinkle resin on the disc to burn.

4. Sit in the quiet and meditate for at least 10–15 minutes. Allow your thoughts to fade away as you get deep into a flow state.

5. When it feels right, pick up your journal and freewrite without thought or judgment. Remember that this is for you only and doesn't need to live up to any standards. Alternately, you can draw instead of journaling.

6. End your ritual and keep what you've created to look back on in the future. Do *not* attempt to decipher its meaning—that's just your logical brain trying to take the reins again. Appreciate the time spent following your instinct and let it be enough.

Worship at the Feet of the Self:
Being Your Own Deity

My own path to embracing witchcraft wound through many years, with frequent long breaks from it as I always got hung up on one aspect: religion. It was when I finally understood witch-craft as a practice rather than witchcraft as a religion that things began to really open up for me.

While many witches are wiccan or pagan, there are many oth-ers that chase a secular path. However, although you may not choose to worship or work with gods, you can still recognize the need to connect with the Divine.

No matter what your worldview is, it's impossible not to rec-ognize the incredible divinity that lies within all of us. We all have that spark of life that makes us magic. The incredible syn-chronicity and fortune in the chaos that resulted in your very existence is divine, and to that end you are special and unique without bounds. Deities are cool and all, but look in the mirror!

A simple way to develop confidence in and appreciation for who you are is to treat yourself as if you are your own god/goddess and create a grounding altar to yourself. This way you have a wonder-ful space all ready for you when you need a magical pick-me-up.

If you suffer from low self-confidence the thought of making an altar to yourself may seem absurd. However, it's important to remember that in order to be a true healer you must first heal within. This includes being open to realizing your own strength and power, despite the bullshit that your inner bully might be trying to tell you. It's a very potent form of growth and rebellion to love yourself radically in spite of that voice.

All around you in the natural world, other creatures live completely unfettered by expectations of what they should be. They live as their nature calls, not beholden to the expectations placed upon them by themselves and others. Strive to live in *your* nature, a glorious creature that deserves all the awe and wonder you can muster. Seems conceited? Screw that. You've tried *not* loving yourself and that certainly hasn't done the trick. See yourself for the incredible, unique being that you are.

So regardless of where your beliefs lie when it comes to deity work, know this: When you look at the stars you are looking at a force that shares elements with you. With every breath you're a miracle of unique existence. Divinity can be found within you, and you deserve to give yourself the freedom to explore this. Be your own deity, give yourself praise, but above all else: Love yourself.

A Grounding Altar to Yourself

To create your own grounding altar, you'll need:

- A space of your own (it can be in a drawer or in a box in a pinch!)
- Objects that represent you (photos, personal items, things you've created, etc.)
- Things that represent your achievements (items from your travels, pictures of your children, tokens of accomplishments, etc.)
- Things that bring you a sense of calm or pleasure (scents, candles, crystals, incense, decor, etc.)
- Things that represent your intentions or higher self (Post-it notes, goals lists, spell jars, etc.)

1. Find a suitable space for your altar. Try to pick a place that won't be tampered with by others.

2. Start setting up your altar with the items you collected. Ultimately, you want your altar to be a place you can go to quickly become grounded, not just to the earth but within yourself. Should you find yourself in tears or inner turmoil, the hope is that you can turn here and find solace through your senses with the items you've chosen to display.

Keep in mind that although traditional witchy tools are great, handwritten notes of encouragement and souvenirs from your own days past have inherent and powerful magic.

Banish Doubt and Impostor Syndrome:
You Deserve It

If there's one thing that levels the playing field between all of us it's impostor syndrome. I don't care how amazing you are, there's a good chance that you've had the experience of peacefully going about your business before getting an unexpected punch in the gut from your own perceived inadequacy.

Impostor syndrome is that annoying nagging feeling that you don't belong in a successful or positive situation. Although it can play out in a number of ways, typically impostor syndrome is characterized by the sneaking suspicion that any success you have is dumb luck, or that somehow you've managed to grift your way into being seen as worthy. At its core, impostor syndrome is the idea that you don't deserve good things. The good news is that since almost everyone has experienced this at some point or another, it's more *common* than it is *accurate*.

Impostor syndrome tends to rear its ugly head as a reaction to things going right. It usually isn't popping up in those less-than-wonderful moments where you aren't afraid of losing something great. This particular brand of fuckery seems to thrive on our limiting beliefs about ourselves and what rights we have to good things. Impostor syndrome manifests itself when all these beliefs are clamoring to be heard—even if what we're actually experiencing proves those beliefs wrong.

Ultimately, it's important to recognize that impostor syndrome is as natural and bothersome as mosquitoes or menstrual cramps. Trying to fight it or lingering on the feelings it brings up is pointless. It's best to just take the monk approach by recognizing it and then moving on.

Now, the important part: You are *you*! Not an impostor, not undeserving—you're you (and that's pretty rad). The twists and turns of your life have led to you being where you're at, which, incidentally, is *exactly* where you belong! The doubts you feel are ultimately a fear of failure and the brain's way of scooting its butt across the shards of whatever limits you've burst through. Although the rallying cry to "believe in yourself!" may seem like empty, vapid inspo-porn, it's actually not any more outlandish of a position than the idea that you're a tricky little minx that enchanted your way into a position you don't deserve. Is it that far-fetched to think that your success might be very well earned?

So the next time you feel the sneaky approach of impostor syndrome, stop for a moment, take a very deep breath, and tell it to move on. You're too great for that shit.

A Spell to Combat Impostor Syndrome

To complete this spell, you'll need:

- A match or lighter
- A yellow candle
- 3 or more small pieces of paper
- A pen
- A small jar or bottle
- Sea salt
- Equal parts of the following herbs for layering (depends on the jar/bottle size): dried chamomile flowers, dried hibiscus flowers, dried rose petals
- A label

1. Start by doing your preferred method of establishing a magical space and cleansing it.

2. Gather your materials and ground yourself to align their energies.

3. Light the candle with the intention of building confidence and courage.

4. On the bits of paper, write down any positive affirmations that can counter the things your own impostor syndrome has told you. For example, if your impostor syndrome is saying, "You only got that promotion because of luck," write down "I received my promotion due to hard work and quality performance."

5. Write down as many of these affirmations as you can. The point is to actively challenge the limiting beliefs you have about your success and worth.

6. Layer the bottom of your jar or bottle with the salt.

7. Layer the chamomile on top of the salt.

8. Add the pieces of paper, either rolled up or folded so there is enough room to fit the rest of the ingredients.

9. Add the hibiscus and the rose on top of the papers to fill your bottle.

10. Write on the label "YOU ARE HERE" in capital letters. Place the label on the side of the jar/bottle.

11. Hold the jar/bottle and think of your affirmations. Think of all the winding roads that led to your success and how they didn't arise from "fooling" anyone; they arose from different choices and actions.

12. Holding the lit candle, carefully seal the bottle by allowing melted wax to drip over the lid.

13. Keep the bottle somewhere you see it often to remind you that you're *exactly* where you belong.

Learn to Love Your Body:
Making Peace with Your Meatsuit

One of my biggest regrets in life is the pressure I've put on myself when it comes to body image. Like many, I struggled with my weight, my health, and the never-ending quest to look "better" (whatever the hell that means) throughout my younger years. The laser focus I put on my body shape and physical appearance not only did a number on my mental health; it also affected my physical health for years to come.

Why do we do this? For obvious reasons, the blame is usually placed on the media and societal expectations. In my own case, being a control freak and a perfectionist definitely played a role as well. There's often a perfect storm of reasons that we have difficulty looking past the aesthetics of our meatsuit in order to recognize the incredible wonder of having a body to move us through life.

Although self-esteem is more than simply what you look like, not accepting your body as it is is a major hit to your overall confidence. This goes beyond simply the idea that our shape or weight is a problem. Disability, chronic illness flare-ups, aging, and other factors can also play a role in the push-and-pull relationship we have with our bodies and ultimately ourselves.

Body-positive bloggers may have you thinking that you can go from raging self-hatred to radical self-love practically overnight; however, this isn't the case. Blossoming into a state of accepting your physical form despite all its quirks is a whole fucking process. And it starts with dramatically rethinking how you measure the value of a body and challenging the ideas you have about what life would look like if you finally achieved perfection. Your spirit isn't measured in pounds, and if you have a body that can feel pleasure just as much as pain, you should be thanking it instead of showering it with resentment. You'll get better mental and physical results from treating your body with the care and love it deserves. Start taking tiny steps toward self-love, such as recognizing your own toxic attitudes toward your body, and spending time giving it some damned appreciation. After all, it does lug your chaotic spirit around all day long!

So if you want to fix your relationship with your body, you need to banish all the bullshit ideals that you're carting around. It's perfectly possible to love and respect your body *despite* what it looks like, and it's also possible to change what you look like *without* using hate as a motivator. In order to truly heal your relationship with your body, you must commit to being the healer. Most of all, act as if you're truly rooting for your body! You can't expect your "team" to play well when you spend all your time cheering against it. Every so often, take a break from mentally flagellating yourself for not looking like the vision of ethereal, sultry perfection and look down, poke your tummy, and say, "Hot damn, am I ever sorry for being such a dick to you." Learn to love your meatsuit.

A Bath Spell

To complete this spell, you'll need:

- 1 cup Epsom salts
- 2 tablespoons baking soda
- ¼ cup dried rose petals
- ¼ cup dried lavender buds
- A drain strainer
- A pink candle
- A match or lighter

1. Fill your bathtub with warm water.

2. Place the salts and baking soda in your tub to dissolve in the water. Add the flowers, making sure to use the drain strainer (or even a cheesecloth that's tied shut) so you don't mess up your plumbing.

3. Light the candle and set the intention of loving this body that is your home.

4. As you undress, look in the mirror for about twenty-five seconds. Although this may feel very uncomfortable, it's an important part of the process. Allow any thoughts or feelings you have to come and go on their own.

5. Get into the bath and lie down.

6. As you lie in the bath, close your eyes and begin deep breathing.

7. Still breathing deeply, start tensing and releasing your muscles, beginning with the top of your head and working down to the tips of your toes. Tense each body part as you inhale and relax as you exhale.

8. Allow yourself to feel gratitude wash over you for this body, based solely on its ability to feel things, to move, to get around and do your brain's will. Try to really zero in on this feeling; it should feel appreciative of the practicalities of your physical form.

9. Open your eyes. As you get out of the bath, look in the mirror again and still feel that gratitude inside you like a warm flame. Focus on those feelings and how they are so much more valuable than the scripts you use on yourself.

Consider journaling out any thoughts, emotions, or affirmations that came up for you during this spell.

Choose to Be Reborn:
Moving On from Guilt and Shame

If you've been through some shit, you can wind up carrying a lot of guilt and shame you've picked up along the way. However, when moving forward, entering each new chapter in life, it's easiest to do so without all that baggage.

I was a wayward teenager, and like many, I have a collection of years that I'd rather forget. Although my current life is drama-free, and I know deep in my heart that I strive to be a good person, there was a time when neither of those statements rang true. Once I grew up and began to get my life together, I found myself with some heavy baggage from those times. Despite the fact that my life was moving on, I felt myself burdened by guilt and shame from those messy years.

Guilt and shame can be helpful emotions in certain times and doses, but the problem arises when they become a way of beating yourself down for things that have long since passed. Although it can be good to feel remorse or regret for previous bad behavior and pick up lessons moving forward, simply ruminating on the bad so much that you remain stuck in the past is energy wasted. All of that would be better spent working on your future self and making your present something to be proud of.

We all have the ability to be jerks, and the ability to shine. Every one of us has a past—things we are trying to evolve from and things we long to escape. Although it can be hard to recognize from our own perspective, we're constantly in a state of flux, ever-changing and emotionally molting. I invite you to give yourself permission to let your own past go. In doing so, you aren't excusing your actions or forgetting that they happened—you're simply deciding to put them down to make space to do better.

The world is full of souls, some lost and some found, but together we make up the great cosmic soup of consciousness. Whether you were a thief, addict, or liar, you have the potential to move forward and not allow your worst times to define you now and in the future. As long as those experiences were learned from, lingering in the guilt and shame isn't fixing a thing.

Let go.

Every moment is another opportunity to make different choices. Fixating on the past doesn't absolve you; however, choosing to maintain your motion in a higher direction might.

Forgive yourself and choose to start over.

Choose to be reborn, bringing with you the lessons and the knowledge that you gained from the dark times.

A Spell to Help Usher You Into the Next Phase of Life

To complete this spell, you'll need:

For Scrub

- 1 cup granulated sugar
- ½ cup coconut oil
- 2 tablespoons dried rosemary leaves
- 2 tablespoons dried lavender buds

For Spell

- A piece of paper
- A pen
- A white candle
- A small fireproof bowl or cauldron
- A drain strainer

1. Mix all the sugar scrub ingredients together in a food processor.

2. Set up a magical space and begin the spell by grounding and cleansing.

3. On the piece of paper, write down the things that haunt you from your "former life."

4. Light the candle and affirm to yourself that it's time to move forward.

5. Light what you've written with the candle flame, then carefully place it into the fireproof bowl or cauldron.

6. Put the drain strainer in your shower drain to protect it from larger herbs. Turn on your shower and get naked!

7. Once in the shower, use the sugar scrub on your body. As you scrub, imagine that you're cleansing yourself of all the guilt and shame that have been clinging to you all these years. Visualize your shower as being the birth scene, and once you emerge you will be cleansed of those nasty, lame energies.

8. Rinse off the scrub under the showerhead and visualize a white cleansing light enveloping you as you shed your old life.

9. Optional: After you come out of the shower, you can perform a smoke cleansing of yourself using dried herbs such as sage, juniper, or rosemary.

10. Once out of the shower, affirm to yourself that you are reborn from this moment, with the baggage from before fire-cleansed and laid to rest.

Recognize You're Resilient AF:
Reflecting on All the Shit You've Been Through

Feeling uncomfortable things is never fun, but for those who've experienced trauma or other deep-cutting pain it can become a very real part of your everyday emotional experience. *Wake up. Brush teeth. Sob into the void...*

Although we'd all love to be made of rubber band stuff that allows us to bounce back from difficult shit without a second thought, the truth is we are deeply emotional creatures with memory foam spirits that can have us carrying our bad experiences for ages. Now, it's normal to have the urge to flee from the emotional swamps formed when bad experiences press craters into our psyches that we fill with tears. However, there's something quite freeing about the ability to visit those dark places while still keeping your spirit high.

Viewing the hard stuff from your past through a resilience lens can help you appreciate how those experiences formed you, without denying that they sucked. Although it can be challenging to think back on hard times and past traumas, to do so is to see your strength, and to honor the foundation that you've built. What's done is done, and although the pain may linger, you can choose to keep your eyes forward without having to ignore the past.

Part of why it's difficult to reflect on and appreciate the past is that it can feel like you are somehow excusing those painful experiences. Your inherent sense of justice as a human being can have you stuck on the idea that if you move on, you're letting go of what you're "owed" from those past events—an apology, karma, legal restitution. But the truth is that justice doesn't always come, and you can waste a lifetime hanging around waiting for it.

Instead, the wise thing to do is to realize that yes, those things happened, and no, they were not okay. You can give yourself permission to move forward by acknowledging the wounds you have and choosing to focus on how those experiences changed you for better *and* for worse.

All of our lives are peppered with moments that changed us forever. Those things together have woven the unique tapestries of our lives, and to honor those experiences by building your resilience is to move forward without bypassing the past. Rather than allowing yourself to get roadblocked by past traumas, simply acknowledge them for what they were: a series of transformative events that shaped you into the person you are today. Despite the negativity that they may have brought you, you do have the power to transmute that energy into strength for the future. And that can be accomplished by honoring that those things shaped you rather than running from them.

In the thick of hard times, take a moment to look back on what you've already been through and how you've managed to come out the other side, rebirthed into a person who's overcome so damn much, and has the strength to handle much more. All those things that happened, and yet, you're still here! Your past traumas don't need to weigh you down. Instead, they can show you just how high you can fly even after being shot down time and time again. You are strong and resilient. A survivor. A champion. Even when you don't feel it, your past paints this picture.

A Reflection Ladder

For this exercise, you'll need:

- 3 long pieces of string or ribbon the same length as yourself
- A handful of small "charms" you would like to weave into the ribbons/strings (crystals, twigs, flowers, beads, etc.)*

1. Cleanse your chosen items and ground yourself.

2. Tie your three ribbons/strings together at one end with a loop. As you tie, affirm to yourself that even though this will be an emotional experience, you are strong and safe.

3. Start braiding your ribbons/strings together in plait, breathing deeply and thinking about everything you've been through.

4. For each of the truly formative experiences in your life that have weighed on you, braid a charm of your choosing into the ribbons/strings to represent it. Begin with the earliest moments and work your way to the present.

5. As you braid each charm in, breathe in deeply and allow yourself to feel the things that this experience made you feel. Then, exhale and affirm to yourself that this thing is over, and merely a seed that helped you grow into who you are now.

6. Tie the ends of the ribbons/strings into the top loop of the braid to make a circle.

7. Meditate with your braided circle and think of how far you've come, giving yourself mad props for being a survivor.

8. Hang the braid somewhere visible as a testament to what a resilient badass you are.

*These should be objects that you feel "called" to.

Reconnect with Your Mojo:
Awakening the Sexy Siren

There have been periods in my life when I felt like a powerful goddess, and times when I felt like a lonely old turd, long forgotten on the road of life. Although I remained the same person at both times (and all times in between), the difference has been the energy that I had available to reawaken and connect with my mojo.

Your own "mojo" can refer to many things: overall confidence, sex appeal, sense of adventure, and general lust for life—all those things that make life such fun.

The reason why you lose your mojo—your unique spark—is simple: When faced with uphill battles and endless responsibilities, you seek out the solace of a safe existence. And the more comfort you seek, the less likely you are to explore new or exciting things. This also goes for your inner world. As you settle for the safety of standing still, you can find yourself feeling a lack of creativity or drive. You are surrounded by the same things day in and day out, leaving little inspiration from which to draw new ideas and motivations.

Most people don't make reconnecting with their inner spark a daily priority, which is one way that witches are ahead of the game. Those who practice the craft are very familiar with the spark, and many of us chase it by way of ritual and magic. Through these means, we seek to enter a state of gnosis—an altered mental state that feels as euphoric as it does comforting and safe. This is just another way that the craft can be a radically life-enhancing practice; it helps you carve out moments to seek joy and transcendence in an often boring existence.

Although the mundane is an important part of magic, so, too, is magic an important part of the mundane. Even for the non-witches among us, the feeling of magic is a necessity, and it can be found through adventuring, building confidence, and extending a hand to the sexy beast inside. (Damn, is it getting hot in here?)

Now, how do you approach getting your mojo back? You break free. You embrace your sexy side and feelings of confidence and push yourself far beyond your comfort zone. Dig deep and twist that dial inside you, turning your magic way up to an eleven! Although it can be challenging to connect to your authentic badass self when it feels like life and society are pulling all the strings, to make the efforts to connect with this part of yourself will be well worth your time.

To own your mojo is to feel empowered. Perhaps this is putting on some lipstick, or maybe it's setting a boundary with someone close to you. Maybe it's going to dinner alone or riding a bike for the first time since you were twelve. I don't know what chasing *your* mojo looks like, but I'm certain that it doesn't look like sitting around waiting for life to happen. You have one life to live, and to spend it wasting away is a fucking tragedy. Wear what you like, kick off your bucket list, and have good sex. Ask for that raise and speak up when you don't agree with something. After all, the shortest line between you and feeling empowered is to be unapologetically yourself.

Chase your mojo, and always, always make space to live your best life and do things that make you feel good. As long as nobody else is harmed, let your freak flag fly.

A Ritual to Make You Feel Confident and Empowered

To complete this ritual, you'll need:

- Something that you feel confident and sexy in (maybe it's lingerie, maybe it's a business suit, maybe it's a dinosaur costume…you do you)
- An empty space where you won't be disturbed
- Candles
- A match or lighter
- Music that makes you feel sexy as hell
- Dragon's blood incense

1. Put on your chosen clothes.

2. Ground yourself and create a magical space.

3. Light the candles and sit in a cross-legged position while focusing on their flames.

4. Put on the music that stirs a fire within your bones.

5. As you get into the zone, light the incense and continue bonding with the flames.

6. Put the candles in a safe place, because you're about to dance.

7. Literally start dancing like there's nobody looking. Posture, stretch, shake it, get your arms going: We are not here for judgment. You're moving with spirit now, bless.

8. Dance until you feel the spark of joy growing within. Have fun and get rejuvenated AF.

Visualize Your Potential:
Skinwalking Your Higher Self

Although it's important to accept yourself for who you are, there's no problem with recognizing areas that need improvement and working toward those ends. For witches, personal growth and development are consistent goals with no real finish line. There are always ways to learn and grow, and as your life unfolds, your priorities and focus may change and shift. This is normal.

One thing that has helped me immensely with defining what I want to see in my own development is to "skinwalk" my higher self. Basically, this is a technique where you visualize your higher self dealing with everyday, ordinary situations to get ultra-familiar with how that higher self behaves. Eventually, you'll become so well versed in their moves that you can effortlessly put on that higher self like it's a second skin (and I mean that in the least creepy way possible).

A lot of people would probably say that they're into personal growth, but there can be a real disconnect when it comes to what exactly that means, especially if you don't have a solid picture of it in your mind. Anyone can say, "I want to be better," while the disciplined few will take the additional steps of establishing a clear definition of what "better" means to them, as well as the steps to get there and the reasons why that vision of better is important to them.

One thing that can help to bridge the gap between yourself now and your highest potential is self-awareness. If you have a good sense of yourself (including the ability to recognize your strengths *and* weaknesses), this process of visualizing your higher self—and making it a reality—will come easier. Additionally, if you're able to take note of the qualities you admire in others, you'll be even more equipped to conjure up an idea of what qualities you'd like to enhance or nurture in your own life.

By establishing a clear visualization of your higher self, you can effectively catapult your way to becoming that person in your everyday life. Again, this doesn't mean that who you are now isn't acceptable: It just establishes a goal to work toward. You can simultaneously love who you are now in all your flawsome glory *and* choose to keep growing for the sake of living your best life. YOLO, amirite?

So instead of once again running through all that shit you *wish* you said to your coworkers or revisiting that embarrassing thing you did in eighth grade before bedtime, try to visit your higher self instead. You'll be better off for it, and the worst that could happen is that you drift off to sleep inspired to be your best self.

A Visualization Exercise

For this exercise, all you'll need is a quiet place where you can lie down.

First, find your place (I like to do this exercise at night before I go to sleep) and get comfy. Now in your mind's eye, conjure up a vision of your higher self. Essentially, this is you in your most evolved, happy, and peaceful state. What are you wearing? How do you feel? What situation are you in? What are your priorities? The purpose of this exercise is to get you very acquainted with your higher self by visualizing situations and how the very best version of you would react, feel, or respond.

This is about getting your brain familiar with a you that is in the mental and emotional shape you're trying to manifest. For example, if you have trouble with snapping at your kids, you can visualize the same scenarios that trigger you into yelling but visualize yourself responding with patience.

It's important to always visualize yourself in the "end." You can visualize yourself working to get to the place you want to be, but it's infinitely more effective to visualize your higher self as already existing. Moments at the beach laughing, finally running that marathon, playing with your kids without a throbbing angry forehead vein...the possibilities are endless!

Chapter Three

SUMMON
CALM

Trying to stay calm in the circus of functional adulthood is a struggle to say the least. Although there are those out there who're perfectly adept at keeping their cool, the rest of us are completely lost when it comes to de-escalating ourselves when our emotional meters are cranked way up to eleven. Day-to-day life just isn't designed to have a Zen kinda vibe. We're forever on the hamster wheel of trying to work, pay bills, take care of our health, maintain a social life, cook, clean, shop, sleep, eat, parent, stay out of trouble, and stay sane. And we even brag about how swamped we are and nurture our addiction to taking on more. Why? Because we're rewarded by society for acting as little worker bees, ones that are cooperative and content and always on the go. The busier we are in spinning our wheels, the harder it becomes to feel like breaking free is even an option.

The good news is that witchcraft can be the road by which you learn to slow down, find peace, and nurture yourself. Despite what the outside world might say, it's very possible to conjure calm, even if only for a few moments at a time. In this chapter, you'll learn how to do just that. You'll practice patience through a moon ritual, reset after burnout, gain perspective through energy work with plants, and more. It's time to relax.

Practice Patience by Howling at the Moon: Honoring Life's Phases

Have you ever felt the call of the wild, that urge deep down inside you to go stand barefoot in the grass, gaze up into the moon, and scream at the top of your lungs? The moon has a special place in the heart of most people. Despite the surface fuckery we cultivate here on earth, she just keeps on doing her thing, hella unbothered by the trials of humans. The moon is truly a beacon of consistency in a tumultuous world. It's no wonder we've looked to her for guidance for ages.

One of the things we can learn from the moon is patience. She's steadfast in her cycles, and therefore sets a pace that won't be messed with by outside bullshit. Many of us could learn a thing or two from this example. Patience is a virtue and boy do we ever need it in our society of instant gratification. Today you can buy anything with a button, are aware of news and events almost—if not—in real time, and can borrow your way into things you have not yet earned. As a result, it is harder and harder to wait for things, and inconveniences like slower-than-usual Internet speeds feel more intolerable. Part of becoming comfortable with calm and invoking more of it in your own life is to recognize that life has seasons and phases, feasts and famines. And these seasons and phases can't be forced or skipped over, despite your best efforts. By aligning yourself with the natural energies of the moon, you can settle into a calm stride that regularly sheds the old and finds rebirth in the new—in a patient rhythm.

The best part of using the moon as a guiding companion to work through life is that it's a naturally grounding practice. Just the mere act of glancing up and seeing her there can be immensely comforting. Even small children point with glee when she's visible during the day. Although many adults simply forget to look up, a witch's eyes are often skyward.

Although you usually hear about witches in regard to the full moon, the truth is *all* phases have their purpose. No matter her size, the moon shows up shining, inspiring heart eyes and open arms from all of us down below. Girl even has pockmarks all over her ass and still manages to be gorgeous!

There are four main moon phases that you should be aware of. Starting with the beginning of the moon cycle and back around again, different points call for different magic. By aligning yourself alongside this schedule you're forced to patiently work through the phases in your own life. Finding which phase the moon is in is easy: Most calendars have it listed, and there are multiple apps to help you keep track. And if you journal your workings, you can look back and see the transient nature of the things you've worked to move in and out of your life.

So here's to the moon: that wonderful satellite, night mother, and energetic guidance system. What's *not* to swoon about?

Rituals for Honoring the Moon's Phases

Work patient moon magic into your own craft by exploring the following phases and their witchy associations and trying the suggested rituals for each phase.

New Moon

The phase when the moon is completely dark, the start of a new cycle. This phase is good for intention setting and inviting new things into your life. This is also a good time for shadow work.

Rituals to try: Meditate and write a list of what you want to invite into your life during this cycle. Carve these onto a candle or write them on a bay leaf and burn your intentions into the Universe.

First Quarter (Waxing Phase)

This is when the moon is half visible in the sky. As it is the waxing phase (building up to the full moon), it's a good time to get yourself in gear by doing all the things that will help you manifest the intentions you set during the new moon.

Rituals to try: Create a vision board based on what you're focusing on during this cycle. Work backward from your goals to make an action plan of how to get there.

Full Moon

This is when that brilliant lady is shining in the sky in all her silvery glory. This is your time to harness that energy and listen hard to your intuition. Full moons are a great chance to look around and sort out what's good and what has got to go. The full moon has big witch energy, so if you're wanting to manifest something you can get in a real zone here.

Rituals to try: Cleanse your home with incense or cleansing herbs. As you move through each room, state the energy you want to invite and tell the stank energy to GTFO. Put some lidded Mason jars of water outside during this phase to make moon water you can put in baths later.

Last Quarter (Waning Phase)
This is when the moon is half visible again, closing out toward the next new moon. This is a great time to banish, let go, and just generally drop kick all the negativity, clutter, and low-vibe bullshittery out of your life.

Rituals to try: Sit on the grass and think of how grateful you are for the things that you've let go of, and how you've made space for the Universe to fill up with greatness. This is also a good time for banishing spells, housecleaning, digital detoxes, and bath rituals that are focused on *you* and your growth.

Hang On to That Shifty Bitch Called Life:
This, Too, Shall Pass

I've cried many times in my life, but I remember one time in particular that was especially transformative. I was coping (poorly) with a plethora of issues at the time, and it felt as if there was literally nowhere in my life that I could turn just for the sake of catching my breath. As it goes, I found myself in one of those moments where I completely broke down, tired of everything and desperate for a break.

As I sobbed in a corner, a small voice inside spoke up and said, "Eventually, all things change."

Now, you probably hear this from others all the time, but when you get it, *you get it*. Suddenly memories crashed over me like a wave: all the difficult times I'd had before, all the corners I'd sat in sobbing, all the things I'd thought for sure would break me, and how eventually, all those things passed. In that moment, chaos melted away into calm.

When you're in these moments of despair or helplessness, it's challenging to see the light at the end of the tunnel, but the fundamental problem is that you're looking for a light when there may be just a turn. All things change eventually, and that's not to say they get better, but they do become something else, and sometimes that's just enough of a break to cope. Just as you know there will be sunshine after the rain, there will also be more rain, maybe a thunderstorm, and perhaps hail the size of your fist to come and knock you on your ass before the next brilliant blast of light. Life is a shifty bitch, and that's a blessing.

One of my favorite tarot cards to meditate on is the Wheel of Fortune. This card symbolizes the ever-changing nature of life, honoring how the process is the focus of life, not some imaginary happy ending that's delivered from nowhere. When things are bad, it's important to trust that they will be good again, and when they are good, hold on tight because the wheel keeps spinning.

Even in the depths of despair, it's an asset to be able to recognize this cyclical nature of things. Although it may seem like a depressing thought at first, it's actually quite comforting to know that things are in a constant state of flux. It can remind you to enjoy the good moments you get, while keeping a little bit of optimism in your pocket that tomorrow might suck a little less.

This isn't to say that unfettered optimism is your friend. You can allow yourself to be present in the darkness while recognizing on some level that it's simply just the phase you're in. Optimism, dread, and everything in between all have their places. The main takeaway is to maintain balance and trust in the process with patience. Eventually, all things change.

When looking to the natural world you can see just how these cycles go, and potentially learn a thing or two. Throughout the cosmos there's a symphony of birth and destruction, movement and shifts taking place. A wonderful way to keep perspective in troubled times is to think outside your own life to the bigger picture, soaking up the realization that life is so much grander than the everyday things that monopolize your attention.

So although life can hurt like hell sometimes, just remember: All things pass eventually, and for better or for worse, all things change form. Just keep spinning, breathing, and holding on for dear life.

A Perspective-Giving Visualization

For a calming, perspective-giving visualization exercise, follow these steps:

1. Lie down on your bed with your arms down by your sides, or sit in a cross-legged position with your hands on your knees.

2. Begin deep breathing and exercising your grounding techniques.

3. In your mind's eye, visualize yourself where you are from an aerial view.

4. Imagine zooming out of your home, up into the sky, getting a larger perspective of the other houses around with other people in them. Think of how each of those people has their own unique life and troubles.

5. Keep zooming out into the sky until you are above the area you live. Take a moment to think about all the people, animals, plant life, etc. that are living there. Imagine that time is passing and you are getting a time lapse of the seasons changing. What does that look like?

6. Zoom out further until you are above the earth. Visualize the changing nature of the planet, ice ages coming and receding, asteroid impacts, all the many changes that have led to life as we presently know it.

7. Keep zooming out over the solar system, then past our own galaxy. Keep breathing and visualize the serenity and the chaos of the expansiveness of space. Recognize the fact

that everything is constantly in flux here, even if the time span takes years you cannot fathom. Meditate on the fact that any given human life is such a special and unique thing, and the disorder within us all mirrors that of the cosmos.

8. Go backward down through space, over the earth, and back into your own body. Affirm to yourself that you are an incredible cog in the Universal machine, and that as the wheel turns, so do your circumstances.

Go with the Flow:
Letting Go and Accepting the Madness

I never feel more connected to humanity than when life's kicking my ass and I feebly rail against it in all my arrogant human glory. "Why are you doing this to *me*?" I cry into the ether, a very anxious midsized mammal being chucked around by the tides of life.

As sentient beings and the center of our own Universe, we get thoroughly put out when things don't go our way. Although different personality types handle this in different ways, we all have the tendency to go through the stages of "Disappointed Human Experiencing a Good Rogering from the Universe":

1. Anger ("Why me?!")
2. Judgment ("Well, this is bullshit.")
3. Nihilism ("None of this matters anyway.")
4. Begrudging acceptance ("Okay then, so what now?")

And this is because we *love* to look at things in life in an orderly way. We see time as linear, stories as having a beginning, middle, and end, and concepts like justice as being necessary and deserved. However, just because our human brains long for this structure doesn't mean it truly exists. And it's our attachment to this idea of a balanced order to life that makes us particularly susceptible to disappointment...and a whole lotta stress.

Life comes at us fast, and we have a lot of things that are important to us: our children, our careers, our health, and the people we love, to name a few. We can stubbornly get attached to the way we think things should go when it comes to these elements of our world, leading to mega resistance when anything deviates from "the plan." However, when the hectic bullshit of everyday life hammers you like a storm, the secret is to move *with* it rather than resist. Learning to be flexible and find your calm in times of chaos will serve you better than standing with your fists up, screaming at the wind.

But how can you become calmer—and less disappointed?

The key is to have a clear understanding of the fact that some things are controllable and some things are not. Although there are certainly things that are within your scope of capability and responsibility, there are also a metric ton of variables that can swoop in and take out even your best-laid plans. Trying to fight these uncontrollable parts of life is a great way to waste your energy and land yourself in a disappointed mindset. By simply acknowledging that sometimes "things just be like that," and being very stingy with where you put your emotional energy, you'll be better equipped to handle setbacks and curveballs from life. Which will mean you'll be amply prepared, because trust me, it won't be stopping throwing stuff at you any time soon!

Sometimes things just happen, and it's best to ride the wave. Go with the flow.

A Ritual Bath

For this ritual, you'll need:

- A bathtub
- Storm water*
- A candle and lighter or a camp light

1. Run your bath, adding any (optional) herbs, salts, or oils to the water. Add your jar of storm water, recalling the energy of the storm it came from as you add it to the tub.

2. Use your candle or camp light to illuminate your bath. If using a candle with a real flame, make sure to place it in a safe area where it won't be disturbed.

3. Strip and get into the bath. Start breathing deeply to fully relax your body. If it helps, start at your head and go down to your toes, clenching and unclenching all of your muscles one at a time as you breathe.

4. Once relaxed, visualize a forest by a river. The forest is massive old growth, lichen dripping from the branches as the waters of the river flow and foam over rocks. Envision the sunlight filtering through the trees and sparkling on the surface of the water below. Try to imagine what this image sounds and smells like.

5. Now watch the sky over the forest as grey clouds begin to roll in. Although it's an obvious storm, see the trees swaying in the increasing breeze without resistance, carrying on and doing their thing.

6. As the clouds darken, imagine them erupting with rain that picks up momentum. The trees that were swaying are now caught in a big wind that becomes increasingly violent.

7. Your scene is now a full, destructive storm. Rain pelts the swirling river, as the trees are tugged at sharply. The air is full of electricity as thunder rumbles in the clouds.

8. As the storm rages, tree limbs break and mud slides. The river is full of debris that get thrown around and slammed on the rocks. Trees are falling and destructive energy abounds.

9. Now imagine the storm breaking and the clouds parting. As they move on, the sun begins to shine through and things are calm once again. Reflect on how nature remains thriving despite the storm.

*To collect storm water, leave an open jar outside during a storm. Cap it off once it's full of water and store it for spellwork or ritual bathing.

Hip Check a Bad Day:
Learning to Approach Life
As a Collection of Moments

Look, I can be a jerk at the best of times, but I reach new heights of bitchery when I'm having the kind of day where nothing is going my way (which is definitely *not* the best of times). Bad days are certainly par for the course in life; however, that doesn't exactly ease the sting when you're six feet deep in the middle of one and it seems like you can't get anything to go right to save your damn life. Bad days can seriously ruin your Zen, making all your goals to live as your calm best self seem fretfully out of reach.

Bad days can range from mildly annoying (hello, new super-power of dropping anything you touch for the next twenty-four hours) to downright catastrophic (deaths, major accidents, and other life-altering events). A bad day can be a one-off or a land-slide (TFW your bad day becomes a bad year). But at the heart of it, all bad days have something important in common: They are made up of a collection of individual moments—not a life sentence. You do not have to wait until the next day to get a second chance; each moment is its own new opportunity.

In the thick of a bad day it can be difficult to remember this because when your bad moments begin to snowball downward to a valley of despair, it can seem that a bad situation truly cannot be stopped, and the more you try to slow it down the worse it gets. The result is that you become hyperfocused on this experience and can end up carrying around a bad day for far longer than you need to.

Breathe, baby!

Sometimes a valid plan of attack is to stop, take a deep breath, and shout at the top of your lungs: "What an absolute fucker of a day this is!" Your desperate will to yeet the whole day down the drain will have your spirit in mega-resist mode, which does nothing to honor the fact that these bad moments have come and gone and *it is what it is*. Remain calm, and acknowledge to yourself "Just because this day has been full of bad moments doesn't mean you can't salvage it." Shifting your mindset in this way can help you move forward, rather than just continue to wade in the misery. Breathe, and as you exhale, let go of those moments, inviting new possibilities with every new breath.

The interesting part is that it may actually get worse— reassuring, I know, but it's almost as if the Universe likes to poke you one more time just to make sure you know who's boss. However, you've got this: It's just another passing moment. Send the Universe a message back: "Keep messing with me and I'll keep popping back up. Life's a collection of moments, and there's plenty more where these ones came from. My time will come!"

So although it may feel very woo-woo to say that keeping a positive vibe can help you combat a bad day, the truth is that this isn't that "out there" after all.

If you're having a bad day, recognize that you have options: (A) to keep falling down a negativity spiral and turn a bad day into something even worse, or (B) to take a deep breath and realize that not all bad days are made up of only bad moments; at some point, things do have the potential to turn around—

if you let them. Take a walk in the woods, do some grounding exercises, bake a cake, paint a picture...just try to use a few moments to snap out of it and change the course of the day. Worst-case scenario, the day continues to suck but you had a nice break. That's a risk that's very worth taking.

Bad days are a collection of bad moments. Once they've come, let them go and move on to the next, potentially better moment.

A Releasing Spell

To complete this spell, you'll need:

- A piece of paper
- Scissors
- A pen
- A small cup of water
- A small pot or seed-starting cup
- Potting mix
- Seeds (sweet pea works well)

1. Do some grounding and cleansing.

2. Cut the paper into small strips (approximately the size of fortune cookie fortunes) and on each one, write down something that made your day rough. Look at each of these as part of a collection of impermanent moments.

3. Put the papers into the cup of water.

4. Fill the seed cup or small pot with the potting mix.

5. Plant your seeds in the potting mix and state the following: "With these seeds, I plant new fortune, watered with the sorrows of today."

6. Water the seeds with the water in the cup, then dispose of any excess, as well as the paper.

7. Look forward to better moments and better days ahead.

Get a Little Green and Dirty:
Working with the Energies of Plants

A deep connection to and reverence for nature is one of the main cornerstones of witchcraft. Just as we are all connected in the web of life, plants are also caught up in this, and they can act as our direct link to the natural world. To this end, many witches keep plants, visit the outdoors often, and attempt to work with the natural energies of plants.

As a skeptic and science-seeking witch, it was more difficult for me to swallow this idea of plant energies at first. Honestly, it sounded a little out there. But if you are feeling unconvinced yourself, I assure you that I'm dead serious when I urge you to get down with the energies of plants. Stay with me.

Research shows that even for those who don't practice the craft, plants can have clear physical and mental health benefits. Plants have the proven ability to filter the air, creating lots of clean oxygen in your home. A lot of them can also be used for medicinal purposes, like the agave plant and echinacea. But deeper than that, many also see them as having their own unique energies that we can tap in to to bring us peace and harmony. Shamans believe plants have divine and distinct spirits, each with an intelligence and vitality you can learn from.

As anyone who has kept potted plants or a garden can attest to, caring for them is incredibly grounding and can be a practice that promotes mindfulness. Many plant enthusiasts share tales of their plants showing them a direct window into their own internal states, as those who neglect their own self-care can often realize it by looking to the conditions of their plants. Plant-loving addicts and victims of abuse also have stories of how their plants helped them to heal, providing a source of open, non-judgmental love and energy. Sometimes taking care of something else can allow us the space to take care of ourselves. Plus, they're pretty, and some are even edible...mega swoon!

Apart from these wellness benefits, tending to plants forces you to come face-to-face with the cyclical nature of life. There are times of bloom, times of dormancy, and times of dropping leaves, shedding the old to make space for the new. We humble humans can find pockets of calm in daily life by caring for plants, and gain perspective regarding the natural order of things, and our place within it.

Much as plants have the ability to filter the air, I believe that they are also able to filter energies, leaving you with a sense of renewal. Go to the forest then gauge your emotional state after, and you'll see what I mean.

To tap in to the energies of plants it's important to be still. Clear your thoughts, breathe, and take special note of how you feel and what sensations come to you. If energy work is new to you, just think of the feeling that's in the air during a lightning storm, or the weight of the air in the room when people have just been fighting in there. Clap your hands together, or rub them together briskly then part them, feeling the sensation of what happens when you break that tactile energy. These are the sorts of things that can help you familiarize yourself with the sensation of subtle energies. Like any proper witch worth their salt, I always begin my energy work by greeting my plants, and end with thanking them.

Even if you consider yourself to have a "black thumb," you can still reap the rewards of that plant-lover life. Keep trying and learning to care for your own plants, or take frequent visits to forests or parks, where your knack for murdering flora won't be able to keep up with the vast vegetation population around you. Although energy work can be done with houseplants, there's nothing quite like going outside to a wild or natural setting, placing your hands on the trunk of a large tree, or sitting in the grass and allowing your hands and feet to become nestled between the blades.

So if you're feeling a little stressed out, emotionally fried, or disconnected, then go get down with some plants. I promise you it will be revitalizing AF.

Energy Work with Plants

For this work, you'll need a potted plant or access to a yard/ outdoor space with grass, and a calm space to get Zen AF.

1. Sit with your potted plant or in the grass and begin grounding yourself. Envision an energetic mist rising up from the plant/grass and filling the space around you. Say hi!

2. Take some deep breaths and place your hands close to the plant/grass without actually touching it. Make note of the things you feel: Do you feel heat? Coolness? Tingles? Nothing at all?

3. Keep breathing, and close your eyes, visualizing the plant/ grass as the living thing it is. Think of it as glowing with life and energy that you cannot see.

4. Keep your hands close to the plant/grass (but still not touching it) and pay close attention to any feelings or thoughts you get. If you feel inclined, you can begin trying to do an energy exchange similar to the grounding exercises in the beginning of this book: Visualize that the foliage is giving off a cleansing, misty energy, and that you are receiving and cycling it back. Inhale that cleansing energy, exhale gratitude.

5. Always thank plants for their energy after this kind of work.

Find Balance:
Evening Out the Scales So You Don't Land Flat on Your Ass

By far one of the rudest expectations of adulthood is that we should be able to do it all while staying sane, fit, and happy. Have you ever heard such bullshit in your whole life?

If you ever wondered what it would be like to split yourself into pieces and continuously give them away until there's nothing left to even cry for, then modern adulthood might be for you! Side effects include depression, exhaustion, spiritual depletion, and the nagging persistent idea that you aren't doing *enough*.

Between working, parenting, paying bills, getting groceries, trying to have a social life, and fulfilling every other piddly little obligation forever and ever, it's no wonder that people feel burnt out, unfulfilled, and decidedly *not* calm. Under pressure like that, something's gotta give, and unfortunately that something is usually *ourselves*. We typically find ourselves without any time left to chase the things that light us up inside and make us feel whole. And it's a damn shame really.

While self-help gurus will happily say that you aren't doing enough to fill your own cup and that you should "make time" (yep, yet another thing you're doing wrong—nice motivation, huh?), the truth is that carving out time for self-care is a bit of a luxury in the modern world. Not every parent has access to childcare or support, and not every person is in a position where they can let some things slide to prioritize their own care.

Financial challenges, family obligations, chronic illness, and a myriad of other unforeseen issues can be roadblocks to regular self-care, and these are valid stumbling points that can't—and shouldn't—be brushed away.

The truth is, in many cases, the concept of self-care is built on the assumption that you have other supports in place that can allow you the *freedom* to prioritize yourself. However, although that may not be the case for you, it *is* possible to bring a bit of balance into your everyday life. While it may be impossible for you to get out for a solo hike as a single parent with three small kids, what you may be able to do is take a few minutes after they go to bed to ground yourself with nature in your own backyard. And although you may have run out of money to go to that dance class you enjoy, you may be able to run a bath and take some time in the quiet to tip the scales back in your favor and find your calm center after a draining week.

Self-care has been turned into a booming commercial industry, but to find balance between the obligations of life and the little things that make your soul feel better is the most basic form of self-care there can be. While it can seem like a needle in a haystack, balance can be found in everyday life. And taking the time to find it will leave you amply rewarded.

Once you find balance, you're not finished either. Maintaining an equilibrium between the things you *must* do and the things you *want* to do is a constant practice, yet well worth your time. To find your balance is the best proactive measure to keep yourself from falling deep into emotional and physical burnout.

A Balancing Ritual

For this ritual, you'll need:

- 2 small bowls
- 6–10 small coins (pennies or nickels work well)
- A Mason jar full of moon water*
- 2 smaller cups or jars

1. Smoke cleanse your items and yourself and ground yourself.

2. Lay out your two bowls and set the intention that one is to hold your responsibilities to the world and one is to hold your responsibilities to your spirit.

3. Split the coins up into two even piles. (The purpose of the coins is to represent value in a way that is consistent. For example, a penny is always a penny, and each one is equal, and they hold psychological value as currency.)

4. Pick up a penny from the first pile and assign it a task that needs to be completed for responsibilities' sake: for example, going grocery shopping or doing reports for work. Tell the penny what it represents and put it in the "responsibilities" bowl.

5. Take a penny from the other pile and assign it a task for your own spiritual or personal wellness, something you want to do that fills you up. For example, taking a bath or reading a book for an hour. Place it in the second bowl.

6. Keep assigning coins from each pile until you have countered every responsibility with another, more fulfilling task. The bowls should be balanced.

7. Pick up your jar of moon water and affirm that the water is symbolic of your spirit.

8. Pour equal amounts of moon water into each of the smaller cups/jars, one to represent your obligations to the outside world and one to represent your spirit.

9. Drink from the spirit cup and affirm that you are committed to filling yourself up.

10. Pour the contents of the other cup onto the ground (or down the drain), symbolizing the things you have to give away to the world outside yourself, and that it is possible to balance both worlds.

*To collect moon water, leave a lidded jar of ingestible water outside somewhere the full moon will shine on it. The next morning, bring it out of the light and store it in a dark place until ready to use. The purpose is to collect all that crazy, powerful energy the full moon is so known for. Sounds weird? Maybe, but it isn't hurting anyone and best of all it's free, so let's get weird!

As you cross things off your to-do list following this ritual, take the coins that represent those tasks and "repay" yourself. This will be a good visual reminder of whether your spell was successful, because if you only repay yourself from the obligation bowl, then your spell was unsuccessful and you need to keep working on maintaining balance. (Just remember to be kind and forgiving with yourself: Balance is a continual effort.)

Cope with Burnout:
Recharging in Times of Collapse

The term "burnout" gets tossed around so casually you could almost miss the fact that it's an incredibly destructive force that can not only harm your mental health, but also creep into your physical body and encourage actual illness and physical distress. Burnout is far from the "Gee, I'm stressed and could use a vacation" trope. It is insidious, pervasive, and has the potential to cause a lot of collateral damage in your life.

Burnout is defined as an all-encompassing exhaustion that can be born from constantly being placed at the business end of multiple demands and stressors. And if you just read that and thought, "Hey, that sounds familiar," then guess what? You're right! Modern life is a shitshow circus, and we're the clowns.

The truth is that in most cases, modern life isn't set up in a way that allows us to take care of ourselves in even the most basic ways. We are increasingly anxious, depressed, and detached from the earth and other people. A big part of the issue seems to be our ever-advancing world. When you look at the way people used to live, before increasingly processed, automatic, and technological practices, and compare it to now, there is a huge disconnect when it comes to our food, our pastimes, our communities, and our relationships. Like some sort of nightmare, we end up in the constant cycle of work, eat, scroll through social media, sleep, repeat that is everything but nourishing to the body and spirit. We eat junk, watch junk, and barely keep up with the demands that pull us in each and every direction.

The best cure for burnout would be a radical restructuring of life as we know it, but this is more of a long game. In the meantime, to keep yourself calm and whole, the best you can do is to find solace and escape in tiny daily rituals and moments of reconnecting with the natural world. Taking even 5–10 minutes a night to do some grounding exercises can be a light in the tunnel of an overworked existence. So, too, can lighting a candle, taking a bath, and breathing as a radical act of sucking you back into the present moment, and taking the time to get outside, away from your phone and your job.

Conquering burnout isn't a cure that's done in huge, heroic doses. Instead, it's a remedy that's more subtle in nature. You can approach it in many ways, but to be creative, curious, and rooted in the present is to fight back against the stress of the everyday and conjure your own moment of calm. Rebellion against the toxicity of modern life is found in brief moments here and there. When you place your hand on the base of a tree or linger for a moment to smell a rose, you're choosing to break free from the hectic nature of modern life to connect with something more pure.

While we may need to match the pace of the human world to pay the bills and keep food on the table, we also need to keep paramount in our minds the fact that this isn't the *only* reality. The larger natural world is hiding in plain sight, with enough soul-renewing energy to help fill your cup, or at the very least provide the perspective you need that the rat race isn't all there is to life.

A Ritual to Help Reset in Times of Burnout

To complete this ritual, you'll need:

- A quiet place in nature
- A water bottle

1. Go somewhere outside that's quiet and also safe. Always be aware of wildlife (staying at a distance), and don't get so gung ho stomping around off-trail that you disturb the plant life.

2. Place your water bottle in some grass or plants.

3. Find somewhere in this space (within reach of your water bottle) to sit and ground yourself. Soak in each moment in a mindful way as you practice grounding. View any thoughts that pop in like bubbles and allow them to float off on their own.

4. Stir your finger around in some dirt or sand nearby and then trace a line on each inner wrist to symbolize your connection with the land. You are taking a break from all the other stuff that has left you feeling burnt out and unfulfilled.

5. Put your hands around your water bottle. See it as housing all the energy from the land and visualize your connection with the earth as being the one true real thing in the craziness of a world that is full of shit to distract you.

6. Drink the water and affirm to yourself that the energy of being an earthly creature is within you, and you can draw on this power in times of depletion.

7. Thank the land and look back on this moment when you're feeling stressed.

Chapter Four

MAKE

MENTAL

HEALTH

MAGIC

Moving somewhere new, changing jobs—attempting to renovate your life is hard, but all that exterior shit is a breeze compared to renovating the hot mess going on between your ears. Despite being a dramatically important part of our everyday experience, our mental health is something that many of us tend to keep pretty low on the daily list of priorities, leaving our wellness in various states of disarray. From the odd bout of anxiety to the crippling sense of being totally lost in the swamp of your own psyche, we all have unique challenges that affect our mental wellness, and this is where the important work lies if you want to level up your everyday experience of life.

Witchcraft is a powerful form of supplemental care that can invite everyday magic to reinvigorate your mind. In this chapter, you'll learn how to summon that magic for yourself. You'll take back control over anxiety, use kitchen witchery to better cope with depression, and spark the flame of motivation. You'll also break up with the past and dance your way to better health. As always, the work of magic is best used as a companion to proper medical treatment and support. Although witchcraft may be cheaper than therapy, never underestimate the power of professional medical care to help you get the tools you need to heal yourself.

Pause Panic:
Managing Anxiety

Have you ever been just chilling when all of a sudden anxiety leaps out like a coiled snake, biting you on the ass and poisoning you with panic while you were just trying to vibe?

Anxiety is your body's uneasy response to stressful stimuli. Although anxiety can be a normal sensation, it becomes abnormal when it starts to infiltrate your whole life, bringing along its heavy baggage of mental and physical symptoms. Clammy hands? *Check.* Obsessively thinking out every scenario that could ever happen? *Check.* The overwhelming sense that you're mega doomed? *Check!* Anxiety will creep up on you when you least expect it, when you *do* expect it, and *anytime in between.*

What nerve.

It is a common struggle, and one that loves to pop up at the most inopportune times. Anxiety has the potential to throw a wrench in your fun gatherings, and panic attacks certainly don't give one single fuck about where you are when they strike like lightning out of the clear blue sky.

Although anxiety is an umbrella term that covers a variety of specific issues and disorders, what they all have in common is an overwhelming sense of dread that'll leave you wishing you could climb out of your own skin. For me, anxiety has always presented as a deep desire not to drop the ball. Somehow my brain got the dumb idea that if I *don't* stress out over every little thing, I'm leaving myself vulnerable to a host of disaster scenarios.

It's wildly exhausting, which makes climbing my way out of it even more challenging. But not impossible.

In my experience, fighting anxiety is largely ineffective. The more I've tried to fight it off, the deeper into a state of resistance I've fallen, which only seems to lead to more turmoil. However, leaning *into* anxiety, while it sounds counterintuitive, can be an effective way to work around it. In this response, you can stand up to your anxiety, acknowledge it for what it is, and make a solid attempt to regain control of your thoughts. I've personally found that the act of choosing to put certain thoughts down for a bit can be a simple way to have a break in the middle of an anxious meltdown. Rather than trying to run from them (or beating myself up for having them), I am acknowledging them, then deciding to take a break before I dive into tackling them. Although this can be hard at first, it gets easier with practice.

If you're struggling with anxiety, it's important to know that there is outside help available as well. There are all sorts of therapeutic interventions and medical professionals who understand the trauma of dealing with anxiety and are more than willing to offer their services. You are not alone. Whatever steps you can make toward improving your mental health are steps in the right direction.

A Banishing Beads Ritual

For this ritual, you'll need:

- A blue ribbon, about 6" long
- 2 Mason jars
- A black ribbon, about 6" long
- A collection of small beads (enough to fill 1 Mason jar)
- A Mason jar full of moon water*

1. Tie a blue ribbon around the mouth of one of the jars, and a black ribbon around the mouth of the other.

2. Fill the jar with the blue ribbon with the beads. These beads represent your thoughts.

3. When you're having an anxious or intrusive thought, take a bead from the first jar and hold it, visualizing it being filled with all the negative energy coming from that thought.

4. As you handle the bead, affirm its task as being a physical representation of that anxious thought.

5. Take a deep breath in and, as you exhale, place the bead in the jar with the black ribbon. Tell yourself that you are choosing to put this thought down. It's not gone, just shelved for now.

6. Repeat this process until the jars are reversed (the black jar is full and the blue jar is empty).

7. Once the black jar is full, pour in the moon water to cleanse your beads, drain that sucker, and begin again.

*To collect moon water, leave a lidded jar of ingestible water outside somewhere the full moon will shine on it. The next morning, bring it out of the light and store it in a dark place until ready to use.

Light a Fire under Your Own Ass:
The Magic of Motivation

Motivation is a funny thing: It seems like when you need it the most, it's not there for you to draw from. Many of us struggle with motivation in various areas of life, a problem that, when left unchecked, can suck us down even further into a lazy hole of "I don't wanna!"

There's also a special relationship between depression and motivation that can leave high hopes feeling like a neglected third wheel. Depression can make even the simplest tasks, like getting out of bed, a monumental challenge. And as the things around you that you *should* be doing start to pile up, your motivation gets trapped under a torrent of neglected responsibilities....It's the perfect recipe for even more depressed feelings.

However, it's not just depression that can hinder motivation. There's a variety of reasons you may feel unmotivated, including personality factors (being the type that wants results and wants them *now*!), feeling underappreciated (such as in workplace scenarios), or simply because you haven't found a good reason to get all fired up and make shit happen.

One of the biggest barriers I've found to motivation is in looking ahead at the whole—the desired outcome. People can often get stuck on this end goal and how far it seems from where they are currently. It's like standing at the base of a mountain, gazing up at the top, and thinking "Fuck, I gotta get way up there?!" It's enough to make you give up before you begin. This is why so many struggle to make healthy lifestyle changes, start new routines, and crawl out of toxic patterns: We're motivated by the end result rather than the mundane actions needed to actually get there.

Although there's no magic bullet for reclaiming your motivation, the truth is that you don't actually need a ton of it in order to make an impact in your life. Big or small, the responsibilities and desires you have are simply collections of items that can be knocked off your to-do list individually. You only need to muster up teensy bits of motivation at any given time to take a step toward getting stuff done. Giving each one of those small tasks your full attention rather than looking ahead at the big picture can be just the thing you need to light a spark under your ass.

Another key to motivation is discipline. Although it would be great if we could look deep inside and find the motivational spark from within, some tasks just aren't the type to fire you up. Many of the tedious things in our lives weigh on us like a wet blanket, and as we avoid doing them due to that lack of motivation, we can end up digging ourselves into a pit that feels impossible to crawl out of. The hard pill to swallow is that sometimes you have to start *before* you're motivated. Begin, and try to dig up some oomph to put behind it along the way.

A Motivational Spell

To complete this spell, you'll need:

- A large lemon
- A sharp object, like a knife or clean thumbtack
- A bottle of cold water or mug of hot water
- 1 teaspoon honey (optional)

1. Do some grounding and cleansing so the Universe can see you're getting down to business and not to be messed with.

2. Hold the lemon in your hands. Picture what your life would look like with motivation. What would you do? What would your routine be? Visualize this as strongly and specifically as you can.

3. Use the sharp object to carve a message into your lemon, something simple like "I am motivated."

4. You now have a motivational lemon. I bet you're the first in your friend group to have an emotional support fruit; congrats!

5. Cut the lemon into slices. If working with a glass of cold water, add a slice to the water, stating, "I am motivated AF; I can tackle anything today." If you are using a mug of hot water, you can add the optional honey after the lemon slice to sweeten your attitude toward doing things.

6. Go forth and get shit done!

Repeat this spell whenever you need a boost of motivation. The lemon is yellow like the sun (a reliable kinda bitch), and its tangy tartness will put a little pep in your step.

Cast Clarity: Using Divination As a Mental Health Check-In

A fun part of being anxious by nature is an overwhelming toxic familiarity with my own feelings. However, despite being cursed with a crippling sense of self-awareness, I still tend to wonder what the hell I'm actually feeling and why. One of my favorite ways of viewing my inner thoughts from an outsider perspective is to engage in divination work.

Divination is the process of accessing knowledge that is typically outside the realm of your perception by way of ritual or magical practices. Every time you watch a movie or TV show where a mysterious crystal ball–wielding woman sees the future, what you're witnessing is a form of divination. There are tons of different ways to go about this practice; tarot cards, reading flames, tea leaf readings, and bone throwing are all forms of divination. However, you don't need formalized tools to do this. Some folks use clouds, water, or whatever else they have available. Hell, you could even yeet some French fries onto the ground and get to interpreting what they mean; I certainly won't judge.

Now, I personally don't believe that when I read cards or flames that I'm communicating with gods or spirits, though this is how some witches interpret divination. As a skeptic and science-seeking witch, I approach divination as a tool to bypass your conscious mind to access something deeper. Have I had experiences that make me think there are supernatural forces at work? Sure, but when it comes to practicing the craft, I find that focusing on the "how" of magic only serves to lessen and dull the results, so I stay focused on the "what." And when practicing divination, the "what" that I am trying to access is the intuitive self.

Everyone has an intuitive self—an inner guidance system. Of course, this deeper truth within your mind can be easily clouded or drowned out by the emotions of those around you, mundane stressors like work, and your own ever-racing thoughts. When I pull a tarot card in the morning to sort out what to focus on that day, or when I meditate on a flame and try to read the shapes, what I'm attempting is to bypass all that other shit and figure out what's truly going on in my head.

Although some people might give you a side-eye when they learn you consult tarot cards or use crystals for scrying, the truth is that this practice can be just as beneficial as any other act of self-care. Doing regular check-ins on your mental wellness is a great way to keep in touch with yourself, and help you decide where to direct your energy each day.

An important part of any divination practice is to look at running themes. If you commonly notice things that are fear-based or feature some sort of guilt or shame, perhaps that's your inner self letting you know you have some shadow work to do. If you feel a sense of anxiety or urgency, maybe your intuitive self is picking up on something that you haven't been able to focus on yet but should. Through paying attention to your gut reactions while divining, you're able to uncover the deeper parts of yourself that may have something important to say.

It doesn't take much time, effort, or materials to do a daily divination check-in that can help gauge where you're at from one day to the next. Although you likely won't be getting winning lotto numbers or solid answers to life's bigger questions, what you may gain is valuable insight into the way your inner self is feeling, which can help lead you through life feeling more in control and supported.

Scrying Your Inner Neuroses

For this divination practice, you'll need:

- A tarot deck
- A notebook and pen

1. Each morning pull a tarot card.
2. Record any emotions or imagery the card brings up for you, as well as your intuitive gut reaction to the card and how it may relate to your current life circumstances.

Consider also looking into further description of what the card "means" traditionally. Pay close attention to how your gut reacts to this information. For example, if you pull The Tower card and your gut jumps to interpreting it as a warning, this is valuable information about your state of mind. (Before applying this information, try to determine whether your gut reaction is a fear/anxious response or if it's actually representative of repressed emotions you might be having.)

Although this task is quick, it can be a great glimpse into what you're feeling at a certain point in life. If you keep track of your cards and interpretations each day in your notebook, you may start to notice patterns, and will end up with a helpful record of what's going on in your life. An added bonus is that over time you will develop a strong working relationship with your deck and will better learn the meanings of the cards.

Get Down with Your "Bad" Self: The Necessity of Shadow Work

One of the things that separates modern witchcraft from your average "love and light" type of spirituality is the obsession with the shadow. As healers, nature worshippers, and seekers of wisdom, witches tend to have a raging spirit-boner for the shadow self that lies deep down, buried within each of us.

If you're unfamiliar with the concept of the shadow (as described by Jungian psychology), it's essentially the idea that we all have a self that we are aware of and show to others, and a darker "shadow" self. This shadow is made up of things that we may not know about ourselves, or bits of the self that we repress in order to fit into society. Your shadow can include both negative and positive traits, such as honesty and implicit biases.

Now, we all have aspects of the self that we choose to suppress and deny. Although this can help us assimilate socially, ignoring these facets of the self doesn't mean they don't exist (despite the fact that we might keep them so hidden that we're often fully able to convince ourselves that we don't even have them). And the truth is that having those repressed sides can actually become harmful. Just because you look away doesn't mean it's not there, and much like stress or anger, these qualities will leak out in the most obnoxious ways—and often at the most inopportune times—to ensure that their presence is known. This can look like projecting your own shit onto others, slipping into bad behavior that surprises even you, and the development of unhealthy neuroses.

The best way to develop a healthy, integrated self is to do some shadow work. Shadow work occurs when you delve deep into those hidden parts of yourself in order to know yourself better. It's like the adult equivalent of cranking a jack-in-the-box toy: Maybe it's a fun surprise; maybe it's terrifying. Either way, it reveals what's dying to get out.

We're all imperfect beings, and in acknowledging even our worst traits and tendencies, we can come to a greater understanding of ourselves, our patterns, and why we do the things we do. Additionally, shadow work can be immensely helpful for those who have issues stemming from hurt and trauma, as it can help you acknowledge the wounds therein and examine their roots in order to move forward to a place of healing.

A person whose spirituality involves the willingness to get deep down and dirty will be infinitely better at riding the waves of life than someone who chooses the path of fingers-in-the-ears, good vibes only, love and light, spiritual-bypassing (a.k.a. using spirituality to excuse negative emotions in order to protect the ego) fuckery. So if you're looking to grow as a person *and* empower yourself through witchcraft, then buckle up and take a good long look at your shadow. In the immortal words carved into the ancient temple of Delphi: "Know thyself."

A Simple Shadow Work Exercise

Although there are many different ways to do shadow work, this is one that's fun and illuminating, and also offers a healthy dose of discomfort.

For this exercise, you'll need:

- A white candle
- A match or lighter
- A notebook or 2 blank pieces of paper
- A pen or pencil
- A coin
- A large fireproof bowl

1. Begin with some grounding and cleansing.

2. Light the candle and affirm that its purpose is to light your way.

3. In the notebook or on the paper, make a line down the center dividing the page in two.

4. Think of a person you know well and you have a problem with or don't like.

5. On the left side of the page, write down all the qualities about this person that are favorable.

6. On the right side, make a list of the qualities you don't like about them.

7. Pick up the coin and hold it while you meditate on the lists you've created, thinking about how each of these qualities could also be used in describing yourself. Even if you feel

you don't share these qualities, try to find examples of times when you've behaved in a way that would indicate otherwise. Additionally, think deeply on why the qualities on the right side are so irritating or upsetting to you.

8. On another page, write the following: "I respect and honor both sides of the coin. I am a brilliant and unique blend of light and darkness; in this I find balance."

9. Light this paper and drop it into the fireproof bowl to burn.

10. Pass your coin through the smoke of the burning page, then place it somewhere visible like on your dresser or your altar.

One note: As you do this exercise, it's important to do so with a sense of objectivity. The purpose is to get to know yourself more deeply, *not* to rekindle your anger toward someone else.

Get Your Shit Together:
Chasing What You Want in Life

When I became an adult, I was woefully unprepared. I was a high school dropout, pregnant, had a plethora of mental health issues, and was aging out of an independent living program through the foster care system. In short, I felt pretty much fucked.

But we are rarely as stuck as we think we are. My experiences have shown me that often we simply have a problem with getting where we need to be because we stick to vague ideas of wanting things to get better without taking the time to figure out what "better" actually looks like to us. I spent a lot of my early adulthood wading through this wholly ineffective kind of thinking and was lucky enough to come out on the other side. I have three kids, a psychology degree, have been successful with work and creative endeavors, and the biggest issues I now face in my life are usually my own bullshit.

When trying to get the things you want in your life, it's very important to think of what the end looks like and work your way backward. By breaking it all down, you're able to create a concrete vision of what you want *and* outline a plan to actually get there. While doing this it's also important to look at your motivations too. Do you want the things you want because *you* want them, or do you want them because they will make *other* people happy? Are you chasing things that will help you feel fulfilled, or that's expected of you? It's real hard to keep up your stamina when pursuing dreams that aren't meant for you, so sort that stuff out now.

Once you do have a vision of what you want, make sure you keep it front and center in your mind. What you're essentially doing is keeping your goals accessible in your mind so you're more likely to behave in a manner that is consistent with achieving them. Clarity of goals and knowing what you want in life are like high-level glamour magic: If done correctly you can convince those around you *and* yourself that your rightful place is in the life you've dreamed up.

So get to work! Take the time to get to know your dream life, define your goals, and trust that what you want will happen—it's just a matter of time. And even if things don't go exactly as hoped, keeping your vibes high through the process is always going to leave you happier and better prepared to conquer whatever life throws your way.

Imagine your dream life, and then make it happen. I believe in you!

A Dream-Life Vision Board

To create your own dream-life vision board, you'll need:

- Art supplies (paper, glue, paint, scissors, glitter—whatever you think you might use)
- Old magazines and/or access to a printer
- A poster board or corkboard
- Black salt
- A citrine crystal

1. Begin by trying to think of a few specific things you want to manifest in your life: the things that the version of you with their shit together would have. This can be focused on anything really; it all depends on your current desires. For example, I've done vision boards that include lifestyle factors (such as activities I wanted to incorporate into my routine), "mood boards" that were more about a type of emotional or aesthetic state I wanted to achieve, and general life boards that included things such as jobs and housing.

2. Start cutting out or printing images that represent the things you want to manifest in your life. You can do this as a virtual project on your computer instead; however, there is something very grounding and real about creating a physical piece you can touch.

3. Gather all of your pictures and focus on them one at a time. Affirm why you chose each picture and what it represents. Allow yourself to feel what it would be like if this already existed in the now.

4. Arrange the images on your board in a way that feels right to you. Affix them to the board and decorate with further embellishments if desired.

5. When complete, lay your board on the floor and surround it with a thin sprinkling of black salt. Place the citrine crystal in the middle of the board.

6. Focus on the whole picture of your vision board. Let feelings of gratitude wash over you, affirming to yourself that these things already exist in the future.

7. Place your board somewhere visible so that you can see it and revisit it often.

8. If you feel you need a little extra boost for manifesting your vision board future, carry your citrine with you for the day (a shirt/pants pocket or bra works well).

Remember not to get too caught up in the outcome. Your mantra here is that the Universe knows what it's doing: Trust that things will happen as they should and let go of clingy energies that are trying to claw at your desires. You got this!

Shake That Thang:
Movement Is Magic

One of the biggest leaps from old society to modern day is the difference in physical movement. The dusty cavefolk of old would roam around doing dusty cavefolk stuff like hunting, making their own homes by hand, and just trying to *survive*. Now we spend most of our time sitting at desks, bent over computers, or jagged-necked over our phones LOL-ing at memes and fighting with our neighbors on *Nextdoor*.

Modern life has us so fucking busy with mundane stuff that sometimes we can't even remember the last time we moved in an exhilarating or purposeful way. Instead of physical activity being a part of everyday life, for many of us it became just another thing to fit in while trying to pay the bills and stay sane.

For obvious reasons, this is a bad development in the wellness sense. Desk-dwelling is a huge impediment to both mental and physical health. A whole new industry of standing desks, yoga-ball chairs, and other such Franken-ventions has emerged from this issue, promising to save your ass (literally) without you missing a single moment of work.

Good times.

However, while standing might be better than sitting, it's still not the kind of uninhibited motion that makes you feel *alive*. Movement can be magic—for your mind, body, *and* spirit—and even the most curmudgeonly couch-sitters among us (like myself) can't deny the power of a good stretch, long walk, or shame-free dance in tune with some wonderful music. There's a reason that sacred dancing is a thing, with many religions and modes of spirituality employing ceremonial dancing in their rites. So although we might be in the unfortunate position of needing to fit movement into our schedule, it's important not to discount the importance of actually making the effort to do so.

Now, it's also important to note that motion for one person may look different than it does to another. There's a wide range of variance between how humans are able to approach movement, based on where they're at in any given time. When I was in my twenties I struggled with chronic illness, and my physical capabilities looked drastically different than they do now. It's important to meet your body where it is and not overextend yourself.

And while motivations to get moving might be lacking, the truth is when you find something you vibe with it makes all the difference. If going to the gym isn't your thing, maybe hiking is? Perhaps a little *dance like there's nobody watching* action? Anyone who says they don't let themselves flop around like a ragdoll when they're alone and hear *that song* (we all have one) is a liar.

So if you want to feel reinvigorated and get down with your magical self, then get yourself in gear. Sit up straight, stretch your body, dance, and move like it's your job! Aside from the obvious physical health benefits, you might just find yourself transported to a more mindful, joyful place.

A Dance Ritual

For this ritual, you'll need:

- Music
- A quiet place (either inside or outdoors) with lots of room to move

1. Crouch down and hug your knees, or if your mobility is limited, begin by sitting in a chair.

2. Raise your arms up in the air and stand, if able.

3. Stretch your arms out to both sides, then front and back.

4. Begin to dance, focusing on stretching your limbs and moving in a way that feels intuitive. If you think you look like a doofus, don't worry: You aren't being judged or graded on this.

5. Feel free to bow and stretch to your corners if it feels right. Mimic the four natural elements. Posture like a bird. Get weird and shake that thing. Don't think for one second about dancing "properly." You're trying to unleash your inner rubber band because chances are you spend far too much of your life crunched up like a crumpled burger wrapper.

6. Pay close attention to your physical sensations as you dance and let the music creep into your spirit and jiggle you around as it chooses.

7. Repeat this shit—*often*! I'm the clumsiest trick on the planet and if I can do it, then you can too!

Cut Cords with Your Former Self:
Breaking Up with Your Past

While taking a trip down memory lane can be fun for many, it can also be a monster-filled trek through spooky woods when your past is full of shit you'd rather forget. But although there may be things from your past that haunt you or cause you pain, the important thing is to lift yourself out of *there* and gain your footing *here* (and now)! Spending too much time in your head worrying about the future or fretting about the past is a surefire way to spiral into a negative emotional cycle, especially when that time is spent ruminating on past transgressions and failures.

Part of the reason that many of us struggle to cut ties with our past selves is that we carry the person we were with us through our memories of past experiences. Although we are all capable of growth and change, we struggle to let go of what has happened and be the person that the old us paved the way for. This is especially true in cases where you carry negative emotions about who you once were. This places you in a state of feeling like you need to outrun the past, rather than using it to honor the person you are today.

Another barrier we often face when trying to truly shuck off the weight of our past selves is the fear of how others will respond. It's a natural thing to resist change, and this extends to the changes we see in others that challenge our notions of who they are. Conversely, others might resist changes in us that don't fit the image they have cultivated for us. There are a lot of people out there holding back on living their lives in a way that feels authentic and freeing because they're concerned about how the people around them will take it. The question is this: Who cares?

As anyone who has gone through a transformation will tell you, you may lose some people along the way. But what's the point of living for others when the only one you truly have to answer to is yourself? Like working with the shadow, we can see that parts of us, when repressed, can come out in maladapted ways that cause more damage in the long run. It's better to do your best to be authentic and true to yourself—as long as doing so won't be a source of real harm to others.

So break up with the you that you've been carrying around for so long. That person, their emotions, and all the things they went through acted as a bridge to get you to now. Cross it and move forward, rather than clutching at the posts and remaining stagnant. And if anyone expects you not to keep moving and keep growing, recognize that this is a normal place of comfort for them; keep stepping forward regardless. Those who love you will catch up, and those who don't will fall behind. It's that simple.

Break up with the past that makes you feel limited, scared, and anxious. Accept that those experiences were stepping-stones, but that you no longer have to carry that stuff into the future. Break up with who you were and take your newfound freedom with you into the next phase of living freely and authentically.

A Cord-Cutting Ritual to Break Up with the Past

For this ritual, you'll need:

- A match or lighter
- A black candle
- A 12" piece of twine or string
- A piece of paper
- A pen
- A large fireproof bowl or cauldron
- Scissors
- A large handful of dirt

1. Do some cleansing and grounding to create a magic AF space. Light your candle.

2. Tie your wrists together loosely with the twine/string, with enough slack that you are still able to write.

3. On the paper, write down the things from your past you want to disconnect from: past deeds, events that happened, painful emotions—anything that you want to cut off and not bring with you into the next chapter of your life.

4. Fold the paper into a small square and light it on fire with the candle. Carefully drop the paper into the fireproof bowl.

5. Watch the fire as you breathe deeply. With every exhale imagine that you're blowing out all those feelings, letting go of all that negativity from the past.

6. Use the scissors to cut the twine/string between your wrists. As you do this affirm to yourself, "I cut ties with the things that have been and open up space for the things that will come."

7. Use the candle to light the twine/string on fire and carefully drop it into the fireproof bowl.

8. When the flame dies, take the dirt and mix it into the bowl. Dump the mixture into a flowerpot or garden and set the intention that the bad shit of the past will help birth the good shit of the future.

Feed the Sad Witch:
Kitchen Witchery for Depression Bitchery

Despite the fact that I've spent most of my adult life making jokes about depression, I can tell you with all seriousness that depression is not funny. I've lost much of my life to depression; it's landed me in the hospital, in bed for days on end, trapped in my house, and raging against those who've loved me. Depression has stolen countless moments from my family as I've struggled to regain control, and the jokes just help me cope with the fear that at any given moment, this beast could rise again and pull me under.

The truth is depression just doesn't *care*. Things can be chugging away as normal when it suddenly rears its ugly head to ruin your day, and maybe even the next few months, with total indifference. Depression sucks. And it can make your life feel like a whole goddamn mess.

When you're struggling mentally, finding the energy and willpower to make sure your basic needs are met can be a challenge. This can include things like eating, showering, seeing other humans, and doing those responsible things we *need* to do like working, paying bills, and running errands without having a breakdown. Bless every grocery store checker who made the grave mistake of asking me how I was doing in those dark times.

Although there are no cures for depression, there are ways that you can cope with it better. Much like with anxiety, I've found that leaning into those bad feelings is a better way to heal than trying to resist or outrun them. But the very biggest thing you can do for yourself when having a depressed episode is to treat yourself like a toddler.

As a mom I can say with certainty that toddlers are annoying AF. They drive you crazy on a regular basis, and demand all of your time and energy—always. Yet we tolerate it all because we understand that they are limited by their age, experience, and cognitive ability. We forgive the frustrating bits and take care of them, love them, and focus on meeting their needs so they have a proper foundation for developing in more advanced ways.

Imagine if we all treated ourselves like toddlers when we were up to our necks in the swamp of depression. We would see that we are limited and need to have our very basic needs met first in order to tackle the higher-level shit that life wants to throw at us. We would be gentler with ourselves, feed ourselves more nourishing foods, and enforce the boundaries that would help us succeed—like allowing ourselves to feel versus just wallowing.

How does this tie into kitchen witchery? A kitchen witch is one who operates mainly in the kitchen. Their spells often involve food, and their temple is the home itself. Intention setting and mindfulness are part of a kitchen witch's magic, and through this craft we can all learn a thing or two about taking better care of ourselves. By using aspects of kitchen witchery, you can make basic need fulfillment an act of radical self-love— something that is often missing when dealing with depression.

It's important to know that you matter. You deserve love and care, especially when things are tough. You need to eat, stay hydrated, and give yourself the patience and care you would give a toddler. Even if you only have enough energy to give yourself the bare minimum, that's something and shouldn't be discounted.

After all, it's all those little steps that add up to build a ladder you can use to hoist yourself out of the depths of depression.

So stretch, have a glass of water, and go eat something. You never know what light your brain might recognize once some of those lower-level needs are met. You might just find yourself refreshed enough to take on more.

Depression Sauce

This is a "bare minimum" recipe that can fulfill the immediate need of hunger. Best of all, it's freezable, and it can help you out in the future when you're in the muck and struggling to do the little things such as cooking. Much love!

For this recipe, you'll need:

- 3 medium cloves garlic, peeled
- ½ medium yellow onion, peeled
- 2 tablespoons olive oil
- 1 (28-ounce) can tomato sauce
- One pinch each of dried herbs for the things you want to invite into your life (great choices include basil for protection and abundance, oregano for courage, thyme for strength and healing, ground black pepper for warding off bad luck, salt and rosemary for cleansing and protection)
- ½ teaspoon granulated sugar
- Any other preferred veggies (e.g., diced green or red bell peppers, grated carrot, or chopped celery or zucchini)*

1. Cleanse your kitchen, including *actually* cleaning and de-cluttering (not just energetically cleansing). I also like to light scented candles during this step.

2. Set your intention. Say, "I'm preparing this food as a gift to myself because I love myself and I am worth it. I deserve to be nourished and happy."

3. Dice up the garlic and onion. Affirm to yourself that these items are for health and protection.

4. Heat up the olive oil in a large pan over medium-high heat. Add the onion and garlic and sauté until soft, about three minutes.

5. Add the tomato sauce to the pan and stir.

6. Add your chosen herbs. Stir.

7. Add the sugar to sweeten your mood. Stir.

8. Add the additional veggies. Stir.

9. As you cook, allow yourself to breathe deep and focus on the food you're making to infuse it with good energy. Focus on self-love and healing.

10. Add your sauce to noodles of your choice and eat up. Freeze any leftover sauce for another day when you're feeling low, like a gift to your future self!

11. Write about this experience in a journal or day planner and remind yourself that even in the depths of a terrible day, you were able to take care of yourself and accomplish something.

*This can be used as a "clean up" recipe, where you can clean out some of the veggies in your fridge that may not be used for other things before they spoil and add them to your sauce. This is another way to kick up the "responsible self-care" aspect of this activity.

Cope with Sad Witch Season:
A Seasonal Depression Ritual

Although to be a witch is to understand the wheel of the year and that all seasons have their place, this doesn't take the sting out of the darkness that creeps in during the colder months. Seasonal depression can be a very real obstacle to mental wellness, with many of us tucking into our homes and lacking the energy to keep our spirits up during this season of hibernation.

While there are folks out there who're affected by other seasons (or living in climates that aren't impacted by the seasons as much), winter is typically the biggest culprit for stealing our sunshine and replacing it with hefty bags of sadness. The second culprit is the fall, which is marginally saved only by being delightfully spooky. However, the initial gut-punch of the days dimming and the weather shifting can be all sorts of emotional. Everything is grey, which can make us feel pretty blue.

There are arguably things to love in *every* season: The thick sweaters and colors of fall, the cups of hot tea or cocoa while watching snow falling outside your window in winter, and the buds popping forth from the ground in spring. Then there's summer, the eternal lover with beaches, blue skies, and staying up till dark to watch the stars. We all have our favorites (can you guess which one is mine?). And we all have seasons we sometimes wish we could fast-forward through.

When it comes to the winter blues and seasonal depression, the most important thing is to take care of yourself. Your mental health is precious, and there's no reason to suffer needlessly. If your quality of life is significantly impaired when a certain time of year rolls around, you need to haul ass to a doctor or therapist *stat*. Life is way too short to be miserable for entire seasons.

There are also some things you can do at home to help you cope. Try to preplan projects to keep you busy during the winter and get outside as much as possible in the brighter, warmer months leading up to it. Whenever possible, do grounding exercises outside, have picnics, go for hikes, forage the land, get your hands in the dirt, and take the time to watch the sun rise and set. To do these things is to make an imprint upon your consciousness: a collection of feelings and moments you can draw from in the cold core of winter.

Ultimately, to keep track of the seasonal cycles is to practice patience and familiarization with the wheel of life. All things have their time, and all times must pass and give way to another. In times of dark and sadness your mantra should remain the same: This season will pass and give way to another. Recognize the purpose of this season and adjust accordingly.

And what is winter's purpose? Well, in nature, winter tends to be a time to hide and hibernate; however, we humans have it backward: We continue a frantic pace of work and celebration throughout a season that is meant for pulling inward and conserving energy. Add alcohol and in-laws, and boom—it's a recipe for disaster.

At the end of the day, you may not be able to "cure" seasonal depression, but you can learn to understand and cope with the challenges. Recognizing and honoring the energy-inward phase of life that winter represents can help you weather it better. Prioritize self-care, mindfulness, and finding peace and joy in the small moments as you wait for spring.

And as always, be easy on yourself. If you get a little down in the dumps in the winter, it's not your fault. 'Tis the season!

A Ritual to Help You Cope with the Darker Days

For this ritual, you'll need:

- A calming yet uplifting tea (something with orange or lemon balm is a good choice to represent the sun)
- A TV or computer
- A video of nature scenes or exotic places*
- A tealight candle
- A match or lighter

1. In the cold dark mornings, start your day off with a warm cup of herbal tea. If you have a sun lamp meant to help with seasonal depression, feel free to use it while performing this ritual. You will sip your tea as you complete the remaining steps.

2. Turn on your TV (or use *YouTube* on your computer) to a nature documentary that focuses on landscapes, especially sunny ones or ones where the sun is rising. Put it on mute, or mute and then play some relaxing music in the background.

3. Begin to breathe deeply and watch the visuals on the TV/computer screen without interruption if possible. You are trying to get into a zone of complete relaxation, with the sun you're seeing on the screen lighting up the bits inside you that are starved for the light.

4. As you continue to deep breathe, chant in your mind or out loud, "Sunny light in darkened rooms, fill the corners, chase the gloom."

5. Imagine the sunlight on the screen going through your eyes, traveling down the nerves into your brain, and continuing through your body. Imagine that you are storing this light to help you get through the darker days.

6. Light your tealight, imagining that it represents the sun and you are sparking it with some of the light that's now stored inside of you. Meditate on that flame for a bit, feeling the light inside of you that's been stored for winter.

7. As you put out the flame of the tealight, remind yourself of the revolving nature of light and darkness.

*Documentaries that focus on wildlife or nature cinematography (not interviews or hosted by people) also work.

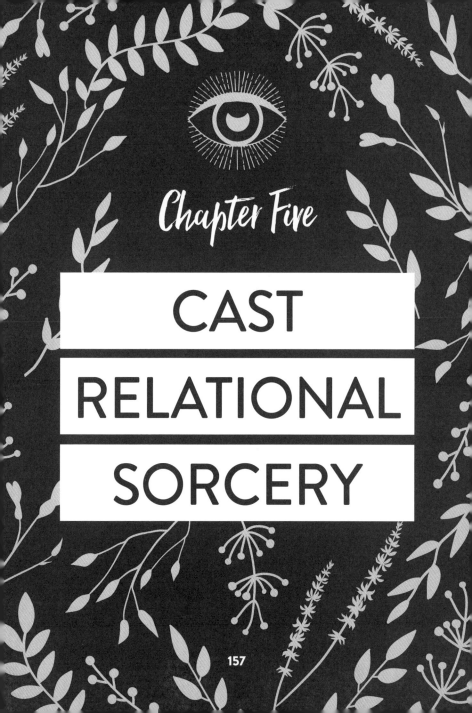

Chapter Five

CAST

RELATIONAL

SORCERY

Each of us has some sort of network of other people in our lives, and these relationships can be simultaneously exhilarating and draining. As humans, we crave connection, and connection brings both good and bad experiences. After all, you each bring your own issues to the relationship. And while you're usually aware of your own issues, when it comes to other folks' shit, it's like tiptoeing around in the dark, silently praying that you're not gonna step in it. Coping with others, whether they be friends, family, or lovers, can be as terrifying and confusing as it can be comforting and fulfilling.

In this chapter, you'll learn how to use witchcraft in navigating the ups and downs of relationships. You'll explore the importance of valuing yourself and bringing more value to your dealings with others and recognize that just as you have agency over your life and actions, so do others. Through a little magic you'll respect their values and boundaries, and work on giving at least as much as you take. You'll also practice rolling with the ever-shifting tides and communicating often, to avoid being swept up or left behind. It's time to enchant your relationships.

Set Boundaries:
Banishing Negativity with Salt and the Word "No"

Of all the things that come along with dealing with other people, boundary setting can be one of the most difficult (yet necessary) things. Boundaries are essentially a set of rules that establish what you *are* and are *not* comfortable with in your interactions with another person.

The difficulty of setting boundaries can vary depending on the relationship in question. For example, setting boundaries with clients or coworkers may feel easier than setting boundaries with your parents or other loved ones. Human relationships are complicated (to put it mildly), and often our fears and insecurities can get in the way of us establishing the boundaries we need in order to feel safe. In many cases, we may just accept the burden of discomfort in close relationships for fear of rocking the boat or losing someone we love.

The thing is, boundary setting is by far the most important aspect of dealing with other people. Boundaries are a way to feel safe and respected in a relationship, and by setting them, you can take your power back in situations where you feel like lines are blurred or roles are imbalanced. They can also help you protect your energies more than any other cleansing technique ever could. Just as we use salt as a means of protection, tossing it here and there and everywhere to straighten out the vibes, so, too, should we be tossing out boundaries like our chill depends on it (because in a way, it does!).

If words are spells, then "no" is one of the most effective spells there is. All too often we smile, acquiesce, and lean down in order for people to walk on us more easily. Similarly, we act out of obligation in cases where it causes us emotional harm (something that people-pleasers especially may be able to identify with too well). By using the power of no, we are essentially banishing all sorts of negativity that we would be accepting otherwise.

Boundaries, baby.

The first order of business is to figure out what your boundaries are. Are certain topics off limits? Behaviors you simply won't tolerate in a relationship? A line you're drawing in the sand about the things you will and will not do? Determine your boundaries.

Although boundaries are healthy, I also want to stress the fact that if this feels difficult that's because it is. The truth is you might upset or offend people, and that's okay. Not everyone has a clear understanding of boundaries, and people get comfortable in the relationship dynamics that have already been established. To flip the script later on does have the tendency to make waves.

And that's okay too.

Just make sure to value yourself enough to know that you deserve to feel safe and comfortable. Be firm in your resolve that you shouldn't have to sacrifice those very important things to minimize the discomfort of anyone else. You matter, your feelings matter, and your well-being matters. You deserve boundaries that are respected. And if all else fails, never forget that "fuck off" is a valid banishing spell!

A Spell for Establishing Healthy Boundaries

To complete this spell, you'll need:

- 1 teaspoon dried chamomile flowers
- 1 teaspoon dried rose petals
- 1–2 teaspoons dried peppermint leaves
- Hot water
- 1 teaspoon honey
- Salt

1. Make a protective self-love tea by putting the chamomile, rose, and peppermint into a tea steeper and submerging in a mug of hot water.

2. Add the honey, stirring in a clockwise direction while stating, "Sweeten my resolve to speak my boundaries into action."

3. Sprinkle the salt in a large diamond shape on the floor, large enough for you to fit inside. Sit or stand within the diamond and drink your tea. Chant or mentally recite affirmations about setting your boundaries, such as "I am strong, I am capable, I am not to be fucked with." Whatever works for you! Gas up yourself enough to truly have the strength and confidence to set and enforce boundaries, so you feel safe and protected.

Break Up with Closure:
Moving Forward by Letting Go

One of the most dizzying, confusing, and rewarding aspects of life on this spinning cosmic rock is the ability to develop relationships with other people. Whether it's friends, family, lovers, or simply other souls whose paths happened to intersect with our own for a moment, we're surrounded with humans we can have both fleeting and foundational interactions with.

But what happens when those connections break down? When things go sideways in a relationship, we often find ourselves burdened with baggage for years, stuffed like a poppet full of loose ends and unresolved trauma. This leaves us emotionally exhausted, skittish, and often obsessing over what the hell went wrong.

Relationships are a funny thing because of their perceived ability to make or break us. The outstretched hand of another can seemingly pull us up from the darkness, or it can be used to yeet us into the abyss. But the truth is that at the end of the day, the only person responsible for manifesting your own happiness and healing is that divine creature you see in the mirror.

This is why you need to break up with closure.

Closure is the idea that when a relationship breaks down, the parties need to come together to hash it out and provide clarity and understanding as to what went wrong. Maybe there's an apology or a cleansing round of tears as you tie up all the loose ends and lay down your pain. Perhaps the gentle rhythmic beat of the local woodland creatures forming a drum circle around you as you hash it out by candlelight, beneath wisps of incense.

Okay, maybe not that last part. But it still sounds great, doesn't it? Almost a little too good to be true perhaps?

The fundamental error with chasing closure is that it operates under the assumption that your power can be so easily hitched to another person's wagon. To hold this perspective is to essentially hex yourself—to remain stunted as long as you stubbornly require other people's participation in your healing.

Let's put it this way: A mountain doesn't beg the river that cuts through it for an apology or acknowledgment of harm. It just keeps on keeping on doing its thing, standing strong and taking ages to wear down and weather. The next river that comes along better cut around or dig in for the long haul. Mountains are the ultimate in resilient energy—repeatedly carved by outside forces yet standing up regardless.

The reality is that people squander years of their lives and loads of their emotional energy trying to conjure up closure that's never going to come. Closure is brilliant in books and movies as a way to wrap things up in a satisfactory manner, but real life is rarely so simple. This isn't to say that closure *never* happens, but you need to start looking at it as a windfall and *not* an entitlement. In real life, people don't owe you fuck-all, and you don't need their permission to cast out the baggage you're carrying. However, if you *do* feel like you need someone to tell you it's okay to move on from closure, then here's a gift from me to you: Put. That. Shit. Down.

Although you *think* you need closure, you feel like it's due and you've yearned for it and dreamed of it being the pivotal plot point in the story of your healing...it's really not. You can both honor your pain and empower your spirit by *letting go* of the desire to have your pain validated by those who've hurt you. You're an empowered witch—a majestic mountain! The ability to stand tall and persevere is deep within you. Break up with closure.

A Spell for Banishing Closure

For this spell, you'll need:

- A black candle
- A match or lighter
- A piece of paper
- A pen or pencil
- A large fireproof bowl or cauldron
- 1–2 tablespoons salt
- A bowl of water large enough to see your reflection in

1. Begin by cleansing yourself and your space in whichever way leaves you vibrating on a frequency that's cozy, safe, and utterly unfuckwithable. Then get to grounding yourself here until you've reached a headspace that feels magic AF.

2. Hold the black candle in your hands. Close your eyes and visualize past broken relationships as open doors in a hallway, with each room housing all the bad feelings that have been left unresolved.

3. Imagine each door closing and energy and a sense of power flowing from your heart, out to your arms, and into the candle.

4. Set down the candle and light it, keeping in mind the intention of closing the doors to unresolved conflicts.

5. Write on the paper your intention to let go of the desire for closure. You can either write about a specific situation(s) to let go of, or even better, something all-encompassing like: "I hereby banish the desire to tie up loose ends for relationships that no longer serve me. I am grateful for the lessons learned and committed to closing doors on old wounds to make space for new beginnings. The power over my healing lies in me alone."

6. Fold your paper, then light it with the flame of the black candle and carefully drop it in the cauldron or bowl.

7. Once the paper has burned, sprinkle some salt in the ash, then pour this mixture into the bowl of water.

8. Gaze into your reflection in the bowl and meditate on the fact that you alone have the power to decide how much baggage you're gonna carry through life.

9. Assure your reflection that although you both acknowledge and honor the pain, you're choosing to let it go for your higher good.

Ward Independence:
Keeping Yourself Whole in a Relationship

Ahh, love. Quite possibly one of the most incredible forms of relational sorcery, finding it is like winning the lottery, except instead of tons of money you get years of putting up with each other's shit.

Now, love *is* incredible, this is true, but if you're not careful you can get lost in it. And the crazy thing is that years of watching rom-coms and toxic TV storylines has us thinking that this is just par for the course in a relationship. As if it's romantic to be lost without one another and put aside everything else just to take up your place as a mere half of a whole. Yowzah.

Not to get all empowerment mama on you, but it's these particular ideas about love that have so many people chasing their tails trying to find it and staying stuck in garbage situations—all for the sake of that flowery, blissful illusion that love can conquer *anything*.

For many years I myself believed in this Hollywood illusion of idealized love—as a struggle meant to pull you under. I didn't love myself or see how that would even matter in the case of a romantic partnership. I was fully and completely the type to lose myself in love, a flaw that remained uncorrected until I grew up, wised up, and decided to spend the rest of my days committed to myself above all others. I'm a better partner for it, and the love I've gotten back since this shift has been beyond anything I could have conceptualized before. To believe that love is something you're destined to get lost in is to seal your fate as becoming just one half of a whole being. And sorry to burst that bubble, but there's no one out there gazing at the stars and wishing to find half of a person to love. People want the whole damn package.

This isn't an attack on love, or a scolding for not being whole enough to be worthy of love—far from it in fact. This is simply a reminder of the importance of keeping yourself whole, which has the incredible side effect of making you a better half to a couple. Although the power of love is dazzling and sublime, quite possibly the greatest commitment you can offer is that of remaining yourself. To bring a whole person to the table, to love and value yourself *first* so that you're more capable of loving someone else is true relational magic.

A Spell to Keep Yourself Whole in Love

For this spell, you'll need:

- A pink candle
- A red candle
- A match or lighter

1. Find a spot large enough for you to sit cross-legged on the floor (can be indoors or outdoors).

2. Begin by grounding and centering yourself.

3. Place the pink candle next to you, and the red candle farther away (it can even be placed on a table or desk across the room; just be aware of fire safety).

4. Light the pink candle beside you and state, "I start this flame with the spark of self-love, from which all else ignites."

5. Breathe deeply and use the energy from your grounding to imagine your body filling with brilliant white light. Visualize it flowing up into your arms and through your fingers. Stand up when you feel full of this light.

6. Point your index finger toward the ground and walk in a circle around the pink candle in a clockwise direction, imagining that you are drawing a circle enclosing both your body and the pink candle with the light coming through your finger.

7. When you are done, visualize yourself in a circle of protection that you've created. Chant, either out loud or in your head, "I am worthy, I am whole, I am my own lighthouse in love."

8. Pick up the pink candle and carefully breach your circle. Use the flame to light the red candle. State, "Self-love to love, and still I remain whole."

9. Bring the pink candle back into the circle and sit with it, imagining that the love you give yourself is like a great well that all other love must spring from. Trust that if you are providing yourself with the kind of love you need and deserve, that romantic love will find you as well.

Communicate Clearly:
Stating Your Needs

If you were to ask my husband what the most annoying thing about me is, chances are he'd say my communication style. Admittedly, communication is not my strong suit. Instead, as a people-pleaser, I'm more the type to pine away in silence about the things I want, simmering into a full-bodied resentment soup before I'd ever let on that I'm upset. This is very ineffective, to say the least.

Whether it's how we were raised or something we picked up along the way, a lot of us have difficulty clearly stating the things we want or need from others. This makes it so that we end up feeling unfulfilled in relationships and unappreciated at work, and we get to a place where we're all too comfortable neglecting what we want for the sake of other people. It's madness!

Despite what we're taught, it's not selfish to try to get your needs met. With the exception of things that would harm others, these necessities are important to being healthy and happy. And many of our needs might actually be met if we just, ya know, asked.

Of course, opening up can feel vulnerable, which might be part of why so many have such a strong aversion to speaking the fuck up. Asking for the things you want or need can make you feel like you're living one of those dreams where you show up to class naked, afraid of how other people will react or perceive you. Although it's normal to find some resistance when you tell someone that you want something they perhaps weren't expecting to hear from you, the truth is that those who love you will listen—if not now, eventually.

At the end of the day, doing what it takes to get your needs met is an act of self-love. This might be exactly why asking for help, or going after the things we want and need, can feel like such an uphill climb. Like many of the things that will ultimately benefit us on an individual level, we allow our own neuroses when it comes to self-esteem to act as a barrier.

Cut that out.

You are worthy. You deserve to have your needs met. You have the right to speak up for your best good. If there are people in your life who contest this, channel your energy into sorting your shit out so you have the confidence and self-respect to deal with this issue appropriately, whether it be through setting boundaries, cord-cutting, or simply moving on with your life.

Value yourself enough to be assertive and get your needs met. No more wishy-washy hoping the other person gets their head out of their ass and reads your mind crap. Communicate clearly and state your needs. It's not selfish. It's not aggressive. It's self-love.

An Assertiveness Spell

To complete this spell, you'll need:

- A rainy day
- A strong wind*

1. Stand outside in the rain and wind and ground yourself, imagining roots coming out from your body and beginning an energy exchange with the earth.

2. Allow yourself to feel the strength of the wind; watch the trees bend and allow the rain to fall on you and influence your comfort and mood.

3. Once you feel as if you are fully a part of this mood, open your mouth and allow the rain to fall on your tongue. Repeat the following phrase, either out loud or in your head, while your head is still tilted: "Just as rain is necessary and good for the greatest benefit, so, too, is my ability to state what I want and need."

4. Lift your arms and stand tall in the wind. Let the wind hit your body, imagining the force as going through you. Store some of that for later; the wind isn't afraid to assert itself, and neither are you.

5. Breathe deeply and see yourself as a part of this force of nature, as all things are connected. Nature has energy you can draw from in times of need, for the greater good.

6. Keep this energy with you as stored strength as you carry on asserting yourself when needed.

*This spell is best done during a light storm.

Break Toxic Patterns:
Busting the Curse

Although we like to fancy ourselves as adaptable and capable of change, the truth is that on a subconscious level most of us are inclined to grow roots into the ruts that have shaped us, dooming us to live out the same bullshit over and over. Unless you remain keenly self-aware and vigilant about checking in with your shadow, there's a chance you might be stuck in an almost imperceptible chain of repetitive fuckery, which can include self-sabotaging behaviors, toxic relationship patterns, and unhealthy roles you take on in your relationships.

How did we get here?

The things that happen to us in infancy and childhood can be very influential for determining who we are and the patterns we seek in life. This can lead to us holding on to the roles that served us in our youth well into adulthood. For example, those who were caretakers as children based on their family dynamic may end up finding themselves consistently taking on that role in later romantic relationships. While this isn't automatically a bad thing, assuming the role of caretaker can lead to an imbalance in the relationship, where one person is constantly giving all of their time and energy, and the other person is primarily taking that time and energy with little return. Some people can even attract the same kind of person with the same set of problems over and over (manifested in different individuals). Without meaning to, we can curse ourselves to repeat toxic patterns with the people in our lives.

However, by learning to recognize why this is and what your role in it is, you can break free. At the end of the day, this tendency is all about comfort. Although it may seem like crazy talk to say that we can be comfortable in maladaptive relationships, the reality is that something doesn't have to be good for us in order for it to be comfortable. It simply has to be familiar. And if you grew up with some heavy stuff that tethered you to the roles you continue to seek out later on in life, it's because your worn-out brain and emotional system see that role as safe. This is why some folks are addicted to chaos: As stressful as it is, it might just be like a warm hug for someone who has become accustomed to it their whole life.

One of the benefits of practicing witchcraft is developing a keen ability to notice these patterns and utilizing shadow work to find out which need each pattern is serving. At the heart of the craft is the desire to heal—both yourself and those around you. To become self-aware enough to tackle the task of breaking these relational "curses" cast by the past is a powerful form of mundane magic.

So how to unbind yourself from these toxic patterns once you *are* aware of them? With love. Self-love continues to be one of the most powerful tools at your disposal when it comes to creating the life you want to live. Believe that you deserve better and allow yourself permission to break the cycle. Love yourself, be careful which spells your words are casting, and do the work on yourself to attract the sorts of relationships you know in your heart you deserve. Explore how your own flaws and habits are contributing to the problem, and dig deep to unearth the root of why certain patterns are a comfort zone.

You are so worthy, and just because something is comfortable does not mean it's safe or healthy. Give yourself the gift of breaking free and cutting the ties that bind you to toxic patterns. You can do this!

Journal Prompts to Help Break Patterns

In a journal or notebook, use the following prompts as a way of exploring your own patterns to determine whether or not they are really serving you in your relationships.

- When I was young, the trait that helped me best survive in my family/surroundings was_____.

- If I had to describe my archetype role in my current life relationships, it would be _____.

- If I had to describe my archetype role in past relationships, it would be _____.

- My biggest fear in a relationship is _____.

- I secretly enjoy the role I take on, even if it isn't best for me, because _____.

- An interpersonal experience that shaped me was

  _____.
  This occurrence is still relevant to my relationships today because _____.

- An emotion that is uncomfortable to me is _____

  because _____.

- Love is: _____.

- The values that I admire in romantic partners and friends are _____.

- In my relationships I am _____ .
  The types of patterns that I seem to fall into over and over again are _____. This keeps popping up because _____.
  (Can you "rewrite" this ending?)

Now, meditate on whether there are toxic patterns that keep manifesting in your life. Create a list of your strengths, and why you should value yourself enough to break the cycle.

Cut the Ties That Harm You:
Casting Toxic People Out of Your Life

As a collective, we probably need to ease up a little bit on brand-ing everything as toxic. Seems that we often rush to label folks as toxic whenever we disagree with them or find ourselves chal-lenged. However, despite the overuse of this term, toxic rela-tionships really do exist. You might even be engaged in some of them, whether you realize it or not.

Legitimately toxic people in our lives can wreak havoc on our wellness. Stress is an illness not to be taken lightly, with many secondary physical and mental health problems that can crop up when you have too much of it. And with interpersonal drama and the stressors that can arise from toxic relationships, you can find yourself drained and emotionally hypervigilant for years to come.

It can be fairly cut and dried when it comes to people who are clearly malicious or spiteful; however, many of us are sur-rounded by soul-sucking relationships that aren't so easily iden-tified. The sad reality is that there are people out there who just love to revel in the shit—miserable people who genuinely have no interest in changing, who love complaining, and who like the feeling of building themselves up on the backs of others. It's a gross quality to deal with, and although we may have a lot of love for that person, we can also recognize that relationships like this are not the best for us.

Sometimes a person needs to be cut out of your life just in an attempt to protect your own energy. If you're constantly being blocked or put down by someone else, their place in your life isn't a good one; likewise if you're being treated poorly, controlled, or put down. Especially if you've taken the time to try to repair the relationship through healthy communication and boundaries to no avail. Some things you just can't fix and your energy is better spent elsewhere.

The first thing to ask yourself when you think you may have a toxic relationship with someone is why you consider this person toxic. Did they challenge you when you were acting like a fool, or did they try to sabotage your life in some way? The first step when identifying negative relationships that are sucking you dry is to check your ego. Is this a real problem, or are you just being problematic? It hurts to go in on yourself like this, but it's a necessary evil. Sniff out the source of your discomfort and set your solutions from there.

Once you've decided you need to cut ties with someone, the best thing to do is distance yourself in a mature way. If the circumstances allow, then you can take the gutsy step of explaining why this relationship isn't working for you, or even simply say you think you'd be better off separating. Although you aren't obligated to explain yourself, it is respectful to do so. Be aware that if you ghost someone, they may decide to paint you as the villain. They would have that right, and it would be none of your business. You're in the business of safeguarding *you*.

If you need to cut ties with a family member, it's a little trickier. Some will say just do it, but real life is more complicated than that. Family dynamics can make a clean break challenging in many cases, so in these circumstances boundary setting and taking space from the person regularly might be your best bet.

Ultimately, to cut ties with someone who is hurting you emotionally, physically, or psychologically is an act of self-love. None of these actions are taken lightly; however, in doing so you are doing yourself a great service.

A Cord-Cutting Spell to Detach from Toxic Relationships

To complete this spell, you'll need:

- 2 sticks large enough to write on
- A pen or knife to write/carve with
- A 24" piece of twine
- A body of water such as a river or stream
- Scissors

1. On one stick, write or carve your name, and on the other, write or carve the name of the person you want to detach from.

2. Tie the sticks together using the twine, with enough slack to hold one stick in each hand.

3. Bring your supplies to a river/stream and sit down beside it. Do some grounding and cleansing with one stick in each hand.

4. Meditate on your relationship with the other person—the good times and the bad. Visualize the negative emotions that arose during your time together as flowing from your hands into the sticks and the twine connecting them.

5. Cut the twine with the scissors, imagining the toxic ties that bound you both as being released.

6. Place the stick that represents the other person in the water, stating, "I wish you all the best in moving forward, free of me."

7. Place the stick that represents you upright in the dirt beside the water, affirming, "I am grounded and ready to take these lessons forward, free of [the other person]."

Transmute Pain:
Forgiveness and Moving Forward

Betrayal is one of the hardest things to deal with in a relationship. Whether it occurred between lovers or friends, the sting is the same, and it can be incredibly difficult to navigate the emotions that come up along with it: hurt, anger, a deep and crushing sadness, and, most gut-wrenching of all, the choice of whether or not to forgive.

Forgiveness is touted as a virtue that does more for the self than it does for the person you're forgiving. Makes sense, right? After all, you are the one who needs to live with the resentment and pain that slid into your life along with the betrayal. Although forgiveness on paper sounds like the right thing to do, even just for your own mental health moving forward, the truth is that forgiving someone is difficult AF.

When wronged, we have a very human tendency to clamor for justice. Nothing activates our thirst for fairness like a big ol' juicy conflict. Forgiveness can feel like a betrayal of the pain you feel, almost as if by choosing to let go you are making allowances for the person and the hurt that they've caused. Within this warped perception is the idea that if you put that heavy shit down, you're dropping the ball on justice. Sometimes we hold on to resentments in a misguided way to honor them or to validate what we felt when we were wronged. To justify the scars and lasting damage we were left with.

Know that when you forgive, you're not necessarily *accepting* someone's actions. You are merely deciding to prioritize your own energies, focusing on keeping them positive. By forgiving, you're choosing to acknowledge that yes, something bad happened, yet you are taking back the reins and no longer allowing the hurt and negativity to take center stage in your heart. In essence, to forgive is to put the hurt down and keep walking, unburdened.

Above all, remember this: You don't *owe* anyone forgiveness, and even if you choose to forgive someone, they don't even need to know. You can choose to preserve your energy through forgiveness, and still carry on your life *without them in it*. In circumstances like this, you are simply allowing yourself to enter a state of resolution with what happened, with your eyes fixed firmly forward rather than behind.

You can cut someone out of your life and you can carry on without them in your circle, but if you choose to forgive, even if it's only for your own benefit, you'll find that you're doing yourself a favor. To forgive is very hard, it's true; but in clearing out those hurts and pains, you're utilizing a powerful form of emotional self-care.

A Forgiveness Spell

To complete this spell, you'll need:

- A piece of paper
- A pen
- An ice cube tray
- Water
- A potted plant or patch of dirt outside

1. On the piece of paper, write down the things that harmed you that need to be forgiven.

2. Tear the paper into little pieces, imagining yourself clearing and releasing all the harmful feelings that were caused by betrayal.

3. Put the pieces of paper in the bottom of the ice cube tray. Up to three cubes should be good. Cover paper with water.

4. Freeze the cubes in your freezer overnight, putting a pause on the emotions that you have been carrying for so long.

5. The next day, take your ice cubes and bury them in the potted plant or patch of dirt. Affirm to yourself that once in the soil, the deeds and the emotions that resulted are cleansed and transformed into something that is positive and renewed.

Optional work: Following this spell, light a candle and meditate on the emotions you want to invite into your life. Do some journaling to help you reintegrate your emotions to aid you in moving forward.

Open the Circle:
Befriending Magic

Making friends as an adult is a fucking struggle. Long gone are the days that you have a built-in friend group based on your age or how well your parents get along. Instead you're now thrust out in the real world and expected to not only meet but also *maintain* friendships with other functional adults—on top of all the other adult things you need to do. It's horrifying! And enough to make you consider not even trying…

However, the fact is that friendship is necessary, even for the most introverted among us. Loneliness is a major side effect of modern life, as we work and parent and do five million other things that keep us *just busy enough* to maintain a sense of isolation that can be incredibly detrimental to our overworked and undernourished mental health. Add a hefty dose of social media FOMO and "nobody likes me" existential dread, and you've got yourself a nice little road map to being down in the dumps. Namaste, fam! Our society puts a lot of pressure on romantic relationships, but the reality is that friendships are just as crucial and can help immensely to break up this loneliness that being a modern-day grownup comes with.

While you can use magic to invite friends into your life, there's also a fair amount of mundane action that's required to back it up. You need to be open to meeting new people and battle your fear or anxiety and get involved in things that take you out of your routine, thus maximizing your chances of meeting new folks.

Now, when making friends, the temptation is to tone your shit down and cast a wide net, therefore broadening your appeal to ensure you can meet more people and therefore make more friends—right? *Wrong!* When making friends, always be your authentic weird self. There's nothing worse than toning yourself down to try to impress another person, and honestly it won't work to keep those friends in the long run anyway. You are leaving yourself with one of two options: losing a friend because you pulled the ol' bait and switch on them, or losing yourself in the fake identity you created to please others. Your best option is always to be yourself from the get-go. Besides, chances are that potential friend you have your eye on is their own brand of weird too. Just give it time.

It's important to have a positive view of yourself when trying to make friends. It makes you appear more confident, which makes you more alluring to others. And to be honest, having a solid foundation of self-worth means you bring more to the table when it comes to creating a healthy relationship with someone, platonic or otherwise.

It's also important to realize that not everyone has to be your BFF. Just like romantic movies often paint over what couples truly are, friendships on TV can also be misleading. Not everyone has to mesh with you in a perfect way, sharing all the same interests and viewpoints. You might find yourself exposed to something new within an unexpected friendship, and this is a very good thing.

Adulthood can be isolating and lonely AF, but by taking steps to meet new people and be open to new things, you'll be able to reap the rewards when you find someone who accepts you as you are. So get out there, smile, and start throwing out small talk like it's your job. With a little patience, kindness, and authenticity you'll find yourself with a social support system that makes life friendlier in no time.

A Candle Spell for Attracting Friendship

To complete this spell, you'll need:

- A pink candle
- A match or lighter
- A few apple seeds
- Tissue paper
- A 6" piece of yellow ribbon

1. Begin by cleansing and grounding, rendering yourself fully protected and ready for that witchy shit!

2. Light the candle and say, "I am enough, I befriend myself, I invite the same from someone else."

3. Wrap the apple seeds in the tissue paper and tie it up in a bundle with the yellow ribbon.

4. Place the seed bundle in your pocket, stating, "With an open heart I plant the seeds to attract friendship." Rest easy that new friendships are coming your way.

Follow this up with real-world action: Be kind, say yes to new opportunities, be generous with your empathy and time, and don't be a jerk!

Attract Love:
Heart Hunting

Let's talk about love.

Love can be many things to many people; however, we're gonna talk about romantic love. You know, that spine-tingling, heart-stopping powerhouse of emotional fuckery that makes people sick kind of thing. They say that to find it is a blessing, but in the deep dirty depths of it, it can feel more like a curse. Love is wonderful and strange and awful all at the same time. It truly is that versatile.

We're indoctrinated from a young age into thinking love needs to be and look a certain way, and sadly the ways it's presented to us via TV and films is almost the exact kind of road map for a disaster you *don't* want to seek. We're sold a lie, and one that causes tons of problems when trying to take those idealized notions about romance and apply them to the real world, where of course they fall short. We expect love to be exhilarating and painful and mind-blowing—which it can be—but then we're left hanging when it comes to real, enduring love, and all the trivial drudgery that doesn't make the silver screen. All too often, people get disappointed by love lacking fireworks, when true, lasting love is more of a slow burn that can illuminate the rest of your days.

Love can be an important part of fulfillment, but at the end of the day, the only way you can attract it is to work on yourself and keep an open vibe to receiving it. Can you find love if your self-esteem is nonexistent and you constantly put everyone else first? Sure, but how healthy would that relationship be? Would it stand the test of time if you grew a pair and decided to switch up the dynamic to be a little more equal?

The hard truth is that you'll struggle to attract lasting love if you don't love yourself. You need to find your own sense of self-worth before you can seek it from somewhere else. By prioritizing yourself, you'll be able to build the proper foundation when it comes to staying independent and being able to establish boundaries. Your head will be in the right place when you realize that attracting love from someone else isn't a cure for the wounds inside of you. You can only fix yourself from within; a potential love interest is not the wrench for the job.

To seek love is to be human. However, it's important to stay rooted in reality and save love for yourself too. To do so will leave you better capable of conjuring the kind of love you seek.

Love is not a catchall, and love is not a solution. What it is, is something far more incredible and wonderful than the movies could ever show. Second only to the love you should feel each morning when you look in the mirror or use your voice to stand up for yourself.

A Mirror Spell for Attracting Love

To complete this spell, you'll need:

- A large bowl of water
- A mirror
- A few rose petals

1. Place the bowl of water in front of the mirror where you can clearly see your face. Add the rose petals to the bowl.

2. Stare at your reflection and visualize love. What does that look like to you? Is it a collection of different moments, an emotional feeling?

3. Place your fingers in the bowl and state, "I love myself above all else; this love will be matched by someone else." The important part here is to realize that the love you give yourself will be a good indicator of what to expect from a relationship.

4. Use the water on your fingers to "wash" your face in clockwise circles. Then take some of the water and do the same to your reflection on the mirror surface. State again, "I love myself above all else; this love will be matched by someone else."

5. Leave the bowl and mirror as they are and repeat this spell whenever necessary, changing out the rose petals and water when needed to keep them fresh. Tell your reflection affirmations of why you would be a good lover.

Match this spell with real-world action: Go out, say yes to new plans and opportunities, give people a chance, stop chasing duds, and have a clear idea of what you are looking for in love (and not some toxic bullshit).

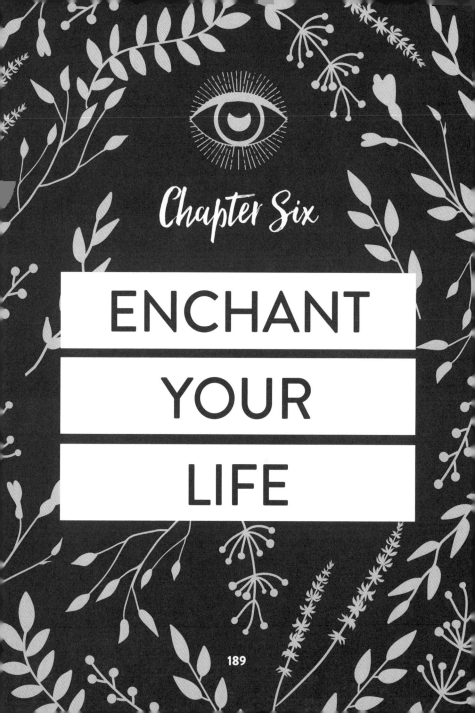

Chapter Six

ENCHANT
YOUR
LIFE

When I was a child, I operated under the very false assumption that adulthood meant having your shit together. I was always a bit naive, but the idea that somehow being an adult came with all the perks like a house, a decent job, and the ability to do whatever you want was a new level of dumbassery. The truth is that adulthood on its own is just a jungle of responsibility with no guidebook on how to navigate it properly and seed it with all the things that will grow into a beautiful life.

Although being a functional grownup can be a bit of a drag, it doesn't have to be all work and no fun. By seeking out moments of joy and fulfillment wherever you can, you'll find yourself blooming despite all the mundane stuff that fills your schedule. Though we tend to equate happiness in adulthood with money or freedom, there are many forms of prosperity and fulfillment you can attract into your life through witchcraft—and this chapter is here to help you do just that. You'll create a bucket list of your must-dos for the future, rethink your assumptions around success, open doors to new opportunities, and more. Just like with most things, the ability to define your goals, be open to new things, and tap dance your way out of your own comfort zone will boost your magic and shape life into a landscape that is equal parts exciting and secure.

Create a Bucket List:
Life Marches On

The world is big, with infinite opportunities of things to see and experience. That being said, many of us go through our lives never tackling the things we wish we could, based on fear, lack of resources, or confusion on how to even start. Part of the problem with the cycle of work-eat-sleep-repeat is that it leaves very little time, energy, and resources to chase the things we truly want in life. This is where the bucket list comes in.

A bucket list is a list of things that you want to do, experience, and see before you...well, kick the bucket. (Shit to do before you die, to put it bluntly.) Although it seems like kind of a morbid concept, it's actually a really neat exercise that respects the idea of your own mortality, honoring the fact that you only have limited time in this realm. A bucket list is a great way to say, "Look, I know I can't do *everything* with the time I have, but here are some of the top things that I feel I would love to do before I'm gone."

Usually when bucket lists are shown in movies and TV, they feature some big travel or experiential component, such as swimming with dolphins or visiting exotic destinations. But the thing about a bucket list is that it can include anything. Forgiving someone or learning a language may be on your list. Even if you haven't ever taken the time to think about a bucket list, chances are you've had fleeting ideas of which things you'd like to see or do before you die.

Now, for some, creating a bucket list might be more an exercise in daydreaming. But for others, this list might be more prescriptive, with the person being very serious about actually seeking these things out. Either way, creating a list of things you want to experience in your life can be a really rewarding exercise for a few reasons. Number one, you might be surprised at the things that you find important (maybe they're more about personal growth than experiences), and number two, a solid analysis of your list might lead you to realize that these things aren't as out of reach as they seem and shouldn't be put off.

I don't personally believe that age has given me too much wisdom, but one thing it has bestowed upon me is the realization that half my dreams were easily attainable if I just got up and started *actually living*. Although I'm sure many people don't sleepwalk through their younger years like I did, thinking anything and everything was impossible, some of us do, and it can be very liberating to be slapped in the face with our own idiocy. When looking at the things I wanted to do or learn before I died, I came to a place of realizing that there was nothing stopping me from at least trying. So, when creating your bucket list, really allow yourself to dream, and most importantly consider this: What if these things aren't actually that far out of reach?

Although it's been the premise of many cheesy movies, there's a lot of truth to the fact that if you knew you had only, say, a year or even a week to live, you would want to spend that time doing whatever it is that you've dreamed of doing. My question to you would be why are you not living that way to the best of your ability even without the firm deadline?

A Bucket List Vision Board

To create your own bucket list vision board, you'll need:

- A piece of paper
- A pen
- Items that represent things on your bucket list (photos, cutouts from magazines, etc.)
- Art supplies (colorful paper, glue, paint, scissors, tape, markers, glitter, etc.)
- A large piece of poster board or cardboard*

1. With your paper and pen, start writing out a bucket list. This can look different for different people; for example, some folks might have "Go to Italy" on their list, while others might have something like "Go one week without a panic attack" or "Try an ayahuasca retreat." There really are no wrong answers here. Your bucket list is as valid if it's simply a mood board as it is if it's a concrete list of "must-do" activities. Trust your gut for what to include.

2. Once you've gathered all your photos and whatever else represents your bucket list, revisit your list and really check in as to why each particular thing made the cut. Be realistic with yourself: Are these things you can tackle soon-ish, or are they things for later in life? You just might find that some of the things on your list are easily doable *now* if you get out of your comfort zone.

3. Arrange your items on the poster board or cardboard in a way that feels right to you. Affix them to the board. Speak each item aloud as a wish to the Universe waiting to be granted.

4. Decorate further with your chosen embellishments. Get creative!

5. Place your board somewhere visible so that you can see it often. Breathe deeply and look at the vision you've made, allowing yourself to see just how possible it is to achieve the things on your list. It might take time, patience, or hard work, but your efforts will be worthwhile. Feel confident in this.

*Vision boards like this can also be done digitally; however, there is something special about going through the creative process and having a tangible item when it's complete.

Each night when you go to bed, visualize yourself actually completing the things on your vision board. Picture it as though it has already happened and affirm to yourself that more than you could imagine is truly possible!

Curate Your Life:
On That Personal Growth Shit

Just as stores perform inventory, we as humans should take some time regularly to take stock of our lives. As we flit our way through this existence, we pick up and drop various things along the way, but rarely take an intentional look around and take note of what's happening in the here and now, and whether these things are beneficial to us or not. Just like our overstuffed closets and junk drawers, our lives may be full of baggage we've accumulated along the way that would be better off hauled out with the trash.

When taking stock of your life in a mindful way, you might just find that there's a few things you're holding on to and you can't remember exactly *why*. People and priorities change, so it's important to check in often and clean out the things that no longer serve you. This is a perfectly natural progression. We need to make space for the fact that that which filled our cups yesterday might be draining them today. This is totally normal growth shit.

Although deciding to give the ax to things that don't serve you may sound selfish and even kind of rude, it's actually one of the best things you can do to ensure that you're giving yourself and the world the best version of you possible. Think of it this way: If you only have so much energy to give and are using it up on things that drains the fuck out of you, what's the point? How likely are you to show up for the things and people you care about if you're chronically depleted?

Although it might seem hasty to throw things completely out of your life, it's a process that can benefit your life in many ways. As long as you aren't using your personal growth as an excuse to duck out of your responsibilities or ditch people who challenge you, you absolutely have the right to examine your life and identify what fits and what you've outgrown. The key is to always be grounded and connected with your reasons why, and not act out of ego, fear, or avoidance. And always remember you're allowed to curate your life in a way that suits you being the best, healthiest version of yourself.

Curating your sphere should be normalized as a regular part of life maintenance, like brushing your teeth or getting your furnace serviced. This process can also look different from person to person, and chances are your gut knows which things need to be tackled first. Social media unfollows, re-examining career goals, and setting boundaries with toxic friends or family members are all recommended, and in doing so you'll be amply rewarded when it comes to your peace and energy.

Although it may sound like a scary process, it's less frightening than it is uncomfortable. That being said, many things that benefit our wellness and personal growth are uncomfortable, and that's okay. You might find yourself feeling all sorts of resistance when it comes to curating your own life: That's just the butler of your comfort zone speaking. Deep down inside most of us love being comfortable and safe, and that inner voice often mistakes a lack of movement for security. The last time I took on this task, I got rid of all sorts of things I spent years building, and when I tell you that voice inside was trying to scare the shit out of me by hollering for me to knock it off, I mean she was *screaming*.

But it's okay.

Ultimately, when you take on the project of curating your life in a way to conserve your peace and energy, you are showing yourself the kind of mundane self-love that's dramatically underrated. You're essentially saying to yourself, "You are worth being happy. You are worth having more energy. You are worthy of living a life that's filled with wonderful things that help you grow and feel nourished." And damn if that isn't just so beautiful.

A Magically Infused Process for Curating Your Life

Follow these steps to curate the things that improve your energy and make you feel at peace and cut out the clutter that drains you. Remember to do this regularly:

1. Meditate on your life presently, starting with your daily routine. Are there habits you developed once upon a time that you no longer need or that no longer bring happiness? Are there things you do daily that are causing you to be energetically drained?

2. Think about your social circle and interpersonal relationships. Are any of these a source of stress, and if so, why? Can these problems be fixed with a conversation, or are these internal issues you can confront through shadow work?

3. Now think of the larger-ticket items in your life. Are you happy with your job? Why or why not? Can this be improved, and if so, how? How about your living situation?

4. Next, revisit your goals. We tend to approach goal setting as a "set it and forget it" thing when really, as we grow and evolve so do our hopes and dreams for the future. Your goals should be as fluid and flexible as you are.

5. Examine the things taking up space in your brain. Are you in need of a digital declutter? Are you stuck in old thought patterns? Have you married yourself to outdated ideas about who you are? Words are spells; are you being a responsible caster?

6. Look around you at the more mundane, tangible elements of your life. Open your windows, clean out your clutter, fill those donation bins with the shit that's simply taking up space.

Tackle Productivity:
You Can Move Mountains
(in a Timely Manner Too!)

Life is a wild ride, but one of the constants is that we only have a limited amount of time; thus we're inundated with platitudes about how we should make the best of it. Although I wholeheartedly agree with this sentiment, my values don't match my behavior when I'm eight seasons deep into binge-watching a show or laid up on the couch after three days of reading ghost stories on the Internet. If we know that we have limited time, and that each day only has so many hours, why do we choose to piss it all away when we could be productive?

Productivity is one of those elusive things that we all kind of want but definitely have to chase. Although you mostly hear about it in the context of work or being a "good employee," productivity is something that affects us all. Getting stuff done properly and efficiently can be a case of how well you run your home, create, or even simply how you use your free hours.

Although it can seem like one of those things that can just sit on our "want to work on" lists, if tackled through intention and routine, anyone can see their productivity blast the roof off of what they thought they were capable of. Productivity can arise easily from being more intentional and specific with your energy, goals, and desires. Think of it this way: Just like we approach happiness or any other vague concept, we center our thoughts about being more productive in too general of a sense for it to be effective. Rarely do we take the time to fully unravel the threads that tie into that goal. What does being more productive mean to you? What does it look like? How do you get there? Like any other goal that has a fighting chance to succeed, you have to begin with clarity and intent.

Now, it might seem like a bizarre and very mundane topic to address through witchcraft, but just like many of life's problems, the barrier that lies between *wanting* to be productive and actually *being* productive is built through your perspective on where your power lies. Are you grabbing the problem by the balls and showing yourself just how capable you are of tackling it by breaking it down and being willing to take a good hard look at your own bad habits and routines? Or are you simply throwing your hands up and saying, "Gee, I wish I could be more productive" then continuing to do sweet fuck-all about it? Words are spells, so what's the script you're reading? If it's a nonstop monologue about how you just don't have enough time to do the things you need and you can't do anything about it, then have fun existing in the unproductive reality you're creating.

Time is limited and you are at a bit of a disadvantage there, it's true. However, you're more than capable of overhauling the habits and routines that govern your productivity if you're dedicated, clear on your goals, and allowing yourself the freedom to think it's possible. Before any other steps, you have to believe that this is an issue you can overcome armed only with your attitude toward it. Because you *can*.

Simple Rituals to Boost Productivity

The following are magical rituals you can use to boost your productivity whenever you're feeling more tempted by the couch than your to-do list:

Casting Intention with Pen and Paper

Get a sticky note or piece of paper and write down what you are going to accomplish today. For example, "I will finish two assignments today, or I will call the pharmacy about my med refills." Affirm this by stating, "And so it is." This is different from a to-do list because you're affirming that it *will* be done, wrangling the ball back into your court. You are more than capable of accomplishing what you've set out to do (provided you started off with realistic goals).

Morning Goal Tea-Stirring Ritual

When having a cup of tea (or coffee) before starting your day, stir in honey or milk clockwise while stating, "I invite productivity into my spirit and into my day." Or, stir counterclockwise while stating, "I release the blocks that stand in the way of being productive."

Shadow Work to Identify Your Dopamine Pathways

Dopamine is a feel-good chemical that the brain releases. It's associated with pleasure and addiction. Many of us are stuck in unhelpful dopamine reward loops, where we engage in certain unproductive behaviors because they flood our brains with the happy sauce. A good example of this is phone use (especially by way of social media or games), which can get in the way of productivity as we get caught in these loops of distraction that are physiologically rewarded. The best way to tackle these habits is to really look into what they are and where they come from. (What need do they fill and why is this need important to you?) By looking into the shadow at the root of why you feel compelled to engage in certain behaviors, you can end up healing more than just the maladaptive routines you've become stuck in.

Attract Prosperity:
Happiness, Money, and Mindset

"Money can't buy you happiness."

Of all the bland, overused quotes that get under my skin, I think this one irritates me the most. What's the operational definition of happiness in this scenario? How much money are we talking about?! Although the sentiment is correct in the sense that no, happiness is not born from money and you shouldn't rely on money being the qualifier to be happy, the truth is that money *does* have the ability to change a life for the better in some scenarios. Maybe you don't have healthcare and are diagnosed with an illness that could bankrupt you? Perhaps you're stuck in a cycle of generational poverty that even a small sum of money could allow you the freedom to break free from?

Although money isn't the main link to happiness in these situations, having it would do a hell of a lot to mitigate the stress and potentially result in an improvement of mood, no? We all know that money can't buy happiness, but as anyone who's experienced poverty can tell you, the value of money goes beyond dollars and cents when it has the potential to make a world of difference in your daily life and wellness. We aren't talking new Corvettes here; we're talking groceries, medical care, and school fees.

If you're involved in circles that are interested in the Law of Attraction and manifestation, the chances are good that you're familiar with the concept of "money mindset." Money mindset is pretty much what it sounds like: the values and perceptions you hold when it comes to money, including attitudes about its place in your life and how available it is. These attitudes are formed by your life experiences and circumstances you grew up in and become more solidly rooted in your self-talk, as the more you tell yourself these things, the more they become your reality.

When it comes to money, scarcity, and the true value of happiness, the way you think about money and your attitude toward it can be barriers to attracting abundance into your life. For example, if you think that money and prosperity are difficult to achieve or are meant for other people and not you, you may be less likely to try something that could be rewarding, or you might fundamentally view having money as a bad thing, subconsciously sabotaging your own money-making efforts.

When I first heard about money mindset, I thought it was a lot of fluffy garbage. It sounded like just the sort of "good vibes only" toxic crap that totally ignores the very real issues that people in poverty face. There's no question that inequity has a huge influence on us, and the thought of money mindset being considered a barrier was completely off-putting for me. However, you can see how those who have enough to be safe approach money differently than those who have always struggled with lack. People who view money as available are more willing to take risks and put effort into manifesting wealth of all kinds in their lives.

I think it's foolish to think that your mindset is responsible for the real-world trauma and difficulties that come along with lower income; however, I will say this: Words are spells. The things we tell ourselves become our truth, and the scripts we faithfully recite shape our realities. What exactly are you telling yourself about money? Are you telling yourself that the desire for money is greedy and negative? Are you convinced that you don't deserve to have more abundance? That if you did have it you would squander it?

To help you answer these questions, I'll leave you with some things to ponder when it comes to money mindset:

- How do you feel about money? Were you raised to think that wanting more was greedy or bad?

- What have you told yourself about your ability to achieve more prosperity? Do you think it's possible, or out of your hands?

- If you are struggling and have come from a history of struggling financially, do you feel stuck in this cycle?

- Have you ever taken the time to define your financial goals?

- Despite feeling lack financially, do you spend time focusing on gratitude?

- Can you commit to ditching the "nevers"? (For example, "I'll never pay off X. I'll never be able to afford Y.")

- Are you guilty of telling yourself you won't be happy unless you have more money?

A Money-Drawing Spell Jar

To complete this spell, you'll need:

- A small jar with a lid
- 2 tablespoons black salt
- 3 tablespoons white or brown rice
- 3 pennies
- A citrine crystal
- 2 tablespoons dried basil leaves
- 6 whole cloves
- A pinch ground cinnamon
- A marker
- A large bay leaf
- A green candle
- A match or lighter

1. Begin your ritual by grounding and centering yourself, then cleansing yourself and your items.

2. Arrange the items (except the marker, bay leaf, candle, and match/lighter) in the jar, starting with the black salt for protection, then the rice for prosperity, coins to symbolize wealth, and citrine, basil, cloves, and cinnamon for prosperity and abundance.

3. On the bay leaf, write "easy money, no harm" with the marker. The reason for this is that you want to be open to receiving money, but under the circumstances that it won't arrive due to harm coming to yourself or others (for example a family member passing, or by a settlement from getting injured). Add the bay leaf to the jar.

4. Light the candle and chant into the flame, "Money flows to me freely, enough to help without the harm. I am open to receiving abundance."

5. Hold the jar. Feel your energy in a concentrated point in your chest that flows outward through your body into your hands and feel it flow into the jar. Allow yourself to truly feel what it would be like to receive money, taking the time to feel grateful.

6. Cover the jar and use the wax of the candle to seal it. Place the jar somewhere visible. (You can also shake that sucker up whenever you feel you need a boost.)

Back up your spell with real-world action like being generous to others, being open to new opportunities, and working on your self-talk when it comes to money and scarcity.

Attract Magical Shit by Giving Back:
Balancing the Scales

As a secular witch, I don't vibe with religion, yet I tend to speak of the Universe as the head bitch in charge of life on this planet. And although I'll never claim to know the true nature of the Universe, I can say that it seems to love balance. The world and all the things in it live in a symbiotic relationship where an imbalance in one place can cause a ripple that ends up needing to be restored.

Witches are particularly interested with balance and evening the scales. After all, when you spend time observing and aligning yourself with nature you can see that the ever-present push and pull of life is an exercise in balance. Balance is key, natural, and a scientific *and* spiritual part of existing. As healers and stewards of nature, witches have a healthy reverence for balance.

One part of balance is giving as much as you receive throughout your life. You have the ability to attract magical shit using the power of generosity. In fact, research shows us that people who are more generous are happier and healthier than those who are not. It's one of those things that just seems to snowball into improving your circumstances. Chances are you've felt this power yourself, if you've ever done something for someone and reveled in the good feelings it brings.

When I think of any success I've gained in my own life, I can usually identify how it has been supported by the kindness of others. Generosity is a simple, low-key way of opening the doors of opportunity, as you're actively taking an approach to life that isn't simply focused on the self. To do good for others is inherently rewarding, but I'd be a liar if I said that it didn't come with significant benefits to the self as well. Generosity is a likable trait that makes others view you more positively, which can lead to better relationships and more opportunities.

The thing about generosity is that it can be incredibly easy. It doesn't need to involve much money or time, and when you think outside the box, you might find yourself coming up with incredibly simple ways to give back in a way that doesn't put you out a lot while making a big impact on others.

Cultivate a gratitude mindset where you can truly appreciate the impact of generosity in your own life. Take that energy and apply it forward in an effort to even up the scales of what you give and what you receive. To do so is undeniably fulfilling, and helps you develop into the type of person you wish to see in the world. Attract the magic you seek by giving back and seeding your magic throughout your life.

A Simple List of Witchy Ways to Give Back

To manifest a balance of give and take that attracts more abundance to your life, try some of the following easy ways of practicing more generosity:

- Use the solstices in the wheel of the year to make financial donations. There are four solstices, and you can use these as opportunities to donate money or goods to your favorite cause (for example, a food bank). It doesn't even need to be a lot; just a few dollars or items can make a huge difference in someone else's life.

- Give back with your time and knowledge. Help a fledgling witch learn the craft or be a resource to those who're interested in the craft.

- Buy from small businesses and enjoy giving support while ending up with a unique and lovingly made product.

- Support other mystics, psychics, and witches by buying or trading readings.

- If you're having a bad day, pay for the meal of the person behind you in the drive-through. It will help break down your bad mood.

- Take the time to understand the viewpoints of others. If you still don't agree, that's fine, but at least you took the time to challenge yourself.

- Go out in nature and pick up garbage as an act of love toward the earth.

- Commit to making small changes for the good of the planet, such as eating less meat or picking up trash at your local greenspaces, even if it's just one at a time for short periods. You never know; you might just overhaul your habits.

- Work on yourself so you are giving the world the very best version of you.

- Always be open to change and new ideas. Don't be stagnant and closed-minded.

Rethink Success:
Defining Your Desires

What does "success" mean to you? Ask this question to different people, or even to the same people at different points across their life span, and you'll end up with different answers. The reason is that success is purely subjective, and our ideas of what it is can change depending on our unique circumstances. While success for some would be defined by having things or gaining opportunities, for others success can be found in the quality of their interpersonal relationships, their own ability to handle the rough shit that life surfs at them, or simply in waking up and being a little bit better than they were yesterday.

It's funny how many people out there chase success without actually being able to pin down what it means to them or taking the time to evaluate whether their ideas of success have changed. In a world that stresses the importance of *School! Job! Marriage! Kids!* we can often find ourselves searching for the success that we defined earlier on in life, even if it no longer resonates with us in the now.

When trying to change your notions of success it's important to take the time to ask yourself what the things you want are and more importantly *why* you want them. As you work through these questions, you might find out that the ways you defined success or decided which things were priorities for you aren't that important after all.

Look, there's a reason for the old movie trope about the person in their golden years re-evaluating their life and trying to come to terms with whether or not they lived in a way that was truly successful. As you go through life, wisdom and perspective put you face-to-face with the fact that perhaps success isn't what's sold to us as eager young folks.

It's also important to get in touch with your higher self when attempting to uncover what success means to you. You know: That badass that's living the life you feel you were destined to live. That zero-fucks-given mad energy put into all the right things in life that you know you could achieve if only you broke free of the ruts and fears and worries that hang heavy over your head.

I've talked previously about this higher self and how important it is to create a model of this person in order to manifest your goals; however, it goes deeper than that. Building a familiarity with your higher self is also key to finding out what your true values are. Stripped of all the expectations you place on where you "should" be or the desire to please other people, what you're left with is that which aligns you with what matters and makes you feel like you're living the kind of alignment and truth that will really set your soul on fire.

What does that look like to you?

In order to find out, it's important to take the time to meditate and visualize the things that are important. The true, deep values that you treasure in your core. To kick it up a notch, try deep cleaning your life of all the noise and things that you're holding because they used to feel important or because someone said that that's just what you should be doing.

Release them.

A Clarity Spell for Rethinking Success

For this spell, you'll need:

- A sharp object such as a thumbtack or small knife
- A blue candle
- A Mason jar full of moon water*
- A medium bowl
- A match or lighter
- An orange

1. Find a place that's free of distractions and cleanse yourself and your tools, then ground and center yourself.

2. Use the sharp object to carefully carve the words "truth" and "clarity" onto the candle.

3. Fill the bowl with the moon water.

4. Light the candle. Affirm to yourself that this candle will light the way for clarity to your higher self.

5. Peel the orange and state, "I carve away the expectations and illusions of success in search of truth and light." Eat the orange.

6. Stare into the bowl of moon water and meditate on your higher self. Dig deep inside that pit of mental chaos to find the core of truth as to what success and happiness truly mean to you. Visualize what those things are and how it feels to achieve them. Give yourself permission to put anything down that isn't a part of this higher self.

*To collect moon water, leave a lidded jar of ingestible water outside somewhere the full moon will shine on it. The next morning, bring it out of the light and store it in a dark place until ready to use.

Use the Magic of Rut-Busting: Opening Doors to New Opportunities

Have you ever noticed yourself falling asleep at the wheel when it comes to life? Spending days and weeks and months doing the same old same old without a thought? Despite being a species that has an insatiable thirst for novelty, we often fall victim to the siren song of comfort that leaves us trapped in ruts that feel impossible to get out of. We end up in grooves that lead us to sleepwalk through life and minimize our chances of experiencing anything new.

I have attracted more abundance into my life by simply switching up my routine than by any other means. Although it sounds obnoxiously esoteric, the reality is that the results you gain from breaking free of your rut are actually very mundane in nature. Your rut limits your opportunities to see or experience anything new, so in shaking things up every so often, you have the chance to both wake up your brain (which has been painfully starved for some adventure) and see, feel, and do things that would have otherwise been outside of your sphere of experience. It's brilliant really.

Now, this isn't to say that routines aren't a good thing. Routines can be low-key magic for enhancing your life and reducing anxiety and can be a practical and devilishly simple form of self-care. However, we can't ignore the value of the unknown and exposing ourselves to new shit. The important thing is to not give your routine total power over how you experience life, and always remain open to taking new roads—even if it feels a little scary or unknown. Because if you're just going to live your life in a bubble then what's the fucking point?

When trying to manifest anything new in my life, I pair it with the mundane action of shaking up the ol' routine like a Yahtzee cup full of fresh opportunities. Driving a new way to work, trying out a new grocery store, or simply saying yes to plans when all you really want to do is sit at home in your pajamas are all small actions that allow you to shake things up without too much stress. A little willpower to break free of your comfort zone is all it takes. Some also see doing this as sending a signal to the Universe that you're ready for new things and open doors.

It's important to remember that just as in nature, balance is key. Although staying in a predictable routine can have many benefits, there is value in the unknown as well, and it's your job to toggle between the two in a way that makes you feel both safe *and* fulfilled. You have one life to live, and you should never discount the power of new experiences and opportunities for filling it with joy.

Sometimes you gotta shake up to wake up!

A Spell for Opening Doors to Adventure

To complete this spell, you'll need:

- A small bowl or shallow dish filled with 1" of salt
- The Fool tarot card
- An aventurine crystal

1. Place the bowl of salt on your dresser or somewhere you can see it each morning where it will not be disturbed.

2. Place The Fool tarot card in an upright position beside the bowl.

3. Hold the aventurine crystal and focus on the card. Visualize roads and doors opening, expanding your experiences and enhancing the quality of your life. Allow all the energy in your body to flow through your hands into your crystal.

4. Affirm at least one thing you can do today to shake up your routine and open your world. Speak it aloud to the card and crystal.

5. Pop that crystal into your pants or shirt pocket or even your bra so it can be your energetic sidekick for the day.

6. Place your finger in the salt and make a line from north to south, then cross it with a line moving east to west while saying, "North to South and East to West, safe paths will open for the best."

Go forth from this spell with intent and magic!

INDEX